On
This
Hilltop

—

For Ruth—
with best wishes

Sue Hubbell

Also by Sue Hubbell

A COUNTRY YEAR
A BOOK OF BEES

ON THIS HILLTOP

— SUE HUBBELL

Ballantine Books · New York

All rights reserved under International and Pan-American
Copyright Conventions. Published in the United
States by Ballantine Books, a division of Random House,
Inc., New York, and simultaneously in Canada by Random
House of Canada Limited, Toronto.

Thirty-three of the pieces collected here originally appeared
in the *St. Louis Post-Dispatch*, 1975 through 1978.
"Factory Women" originally appeared in *Working Woman*
in substantially different form.
The map on page 178 showing the disputed boundary
of Missouri and Iowa is from the collection of the
Library of Congress.

Library of Congress Catalog Card Number: 91-91869
ISBN: 0-345-37306-5

Text design by Holly Johnson
Drawing copyright © 1991 by Don Davis
Cover design by James R. Harris
Cover photograph: "Farm at Dusk,"
Kevin Moan/Superstock, Inc.

Manufactured in the United States of America

First Edition: October 1991
10 9 8 7 6 5 4 3 2 1

For Righteousness
Long May It Wave

CONTENTS

Contents

PROLOGUE

People are always discovering the Ozarks. In the Depression years, the thirties, those with former ties here flocked back, believing that it was better to be poor in the country than in the city. They were followed by rich Chicagoans who came here believing that FDR was taking the world to Hell in a Handbasket. They wanted to hold on to what they had and perhaps, with wily management and the shrewd purchase of land at tax sales, to increase it a bit. In the forties a group of civic-minded local citizens tried, in vain for a long while, to find people who would come here and start a much-needed hospital. The place sounded like the ends of the earth to most who had the skills to do such a thing but the local group, Baptists to a man, found a group of Czech Catholic nuns who came in the spirit of Good Deeds. The nuns spoke little English and no one, as far as I know, has ever established what they thought of the Ozarks, but the local Baptists swallowed hard and welcomed them, as they had welcomed other outlanders.

In the fifties, as you can read in the pages that follow, the flying-saucer faithful descended on the Ozarks, lured by reports of sightings. The local people, some with a chuckle, responded hospitably and sold them the things they needed. Outlanders, by this time, had become something of a cash crop.

The flying-saucer people prepared our local people for the seventies when the young and hip, many of them bummed out on California, discovered that the Ozarks was Where It Was Happening, Man, and moved here with righteous back-to-the-land zeal. A few of them show up in these pages, too. They didn't talk or dress any "funnier" than the Czech nuns and some of them were trust-funders with as much money to spend at local stores as the Chicagoans had, so, by and large and with just a little grumbling, they were tolerated by the Ozarkers. In the decade just passed, military retirees have discovered that a dollar goes a long way in the Ozarks and they've moved here, too.

The Ozarks, however, is a testing sort of place. The ticks and chiggers and poisonous snakes are many and the climate is surprising. It can be twenty below zero in the winter, and the cold weather is accompanied by ice storms that immobilize us all. The thermometer can rise with no trouble to 105 in the summer and offers humidity to match. The Ozarks is a very hard place to make a living. Marriages come apart (mine did), and after the initial grubstake is spent, a cash income eludes most who have no steady source of dollars from beyond the hills. So many of those who thought the Ozarks might be paradise move away. The other evening I was at a party and ran into a man I hadn't seen since the early seventies when I moved here with my husband. He is a some-time poet who does landscape work for people over in the county seat to bring in cash. We reminisced about all those we had known who had lived here for a while and left. "I don't know whether that makes us skilled survivors or just the dregs," he said, laughing. I suppose he'll be at the twentieth-reunion gathering announced in a flyer I received the other day. I hear the nostalgic event will bring back many of the former back-to-the-landers who found what they needed to ready themselves for the next stage (or failed to find it at all) and then drifted on to other parts of the country. It seems hard to believe that it was nearly twenty years ago that I first moved here. Time has passed in the wink of an eye.

Our reasons for moving here were different from those of the hippies, who were much younger than we were, although we certainly shared some of their concerns and interests: distress at what was happening in urban America, an appreciation of the beauty that was here, a desire to live cheaply, certain Maoist ten-dencies and, if these pages are to believed, a consum-ing fixation about growing our own vegetables. Our reasons for moving here were, in part, personal, but in larger part political: my husband was a professor of electrical engineering at the University of Rhode Is-land; I was a librarian at Brown University. Our son had gone off to boarding school at Putney, in Ver-mont. We were involved in the peace movement on all those campuses and my husband and I became draft counselors at our respective universities, helping at least some young men escape service in a war that none of us believed in. But Nixon was king and the war seemed endless. We lamented the fact that the total deductions from our paychecks for taxes was greater than my senior staff assistant's entire salary. And those taxes went to support a war we opposed. The only thing to do, it seemed to us and some others of our belief, was to step outside the wage-earning life and escape the cash economy.

It was impossible, of course, but what follows is a record of our attempt, in reports that I wrote for the *St. Louis Post-Dispatch*, in the mid-1970s along with a couple of longer pieces I wrote during that time. For me they were the beginning of a writing life, one of several I have lived.

Summer, 1990

ON
THIS
HILLTOP

—

THE WEST SIDE MEETS
A MISSOURI CHICKEN

————

October 9, 1975

Friends and relatives think that it is great fun that we have a farm in the Ozarks. They conjure up pictures of husking bees, barefoot boys with cane fishing poles, and healthy outdoor work that tones the muscles and earns the right to enormous dinners composed entirely of apple pie. They are also eager to send us their children to take part in these rosy, wholesome activities.

We were very busy last summer when Bruce was thrust on us by his mother, who lives in New York City. We were building a honey house, working frantically with the bees to keep them from swarming and trying to keep a balance in the garden that was favorable to the vegetables and us rather than the weeds and bugs. "He'll be bored," I protested weakly. I had heard that Bruce was a rather elegant, precocious young man and I tried to picture him whiling away his afternoons at the local pool and pinball establishment.

3

"Nonsense," his mother replied firmly. "He loves to work; he'll be a big help to you."

Our son, Brian, who had met the boy in question, looked amused and said, "It'll be good for him." So I gave in and a few days later we drove to St. Louis to meet him at the airport.

He was a pale, slouching fourteen-year-old with styled hair. He wore carefully rumpled corduroys, a madras jacket and earth shoes. And he carried a cunning, collapsible fishing rod in an aluminum case. He peered at St. Louis from the airport.

"Actually," he confided, "living in New York has made it impossible for me to find any other city interesting."

I suppressed a knee-jerk defense of America's heartland and spent the time on the drive home trying to interest him in rural living. He was fascinated, horribly fascinated, by snakes.

"Actually," he said, "I know all about snakes. I have a very good book on the subject."

He was particularly interested in copperheads. He knew that one had struck one of our dogs a few weeks earlier and wanted to hear the story in detail. I finished by telling him that yes, we did occasionally see copperheads, that they weren't aggressive, but that it was a good idea to wear boots out in the fields and woods, and that it was easy to distinguish copperheads from nonpoisonous snakes with similar markings by their triangular-shaped heads, the jaws being wider than the rest of the head.

"Yes, yes, I know all that," he told me.

Had he ever seen a copperhead? "Well, actually, no," he said. "But I saw a very good exhibit on snakes at the Museum of Natural History. In New York."

The first day that we were home, Bruce went down to the river with his fishing rod. He had not been gone long when we heard anguished whoops. "Snakes! Snakes!" Bruce screamed as he ran up the path from the river. Excitedly, he explained that he had just seen a copperhead. Was he sure it was a copperhead?

"Well, actually, it was a very small one," he said. "It was hard to see the wideness of the head, but I know it was a copperhead. And the scary thing was that it was little, because that means that it is a baby snake and the mother snake will be nearby trying to protect it and . . ."

"Bruce," I interrupted, "I don't think that mother snakes . . ."

"I know all about snakes," he replied firmly. "I read about them in my book. Another thing: This copperhead was sort of hopping along and it made a funny noise."

"Are you sure you saw a snake, Bruce?"

"Yes, it was just like the one I saw at the Natural History Museum."

"In New York."

"Yes, in New York."

Bruce was not keen on going back to the river. He folded up his fishing rod and it stayed in a corner of the kitchen for the rest of his visit.

The next day, I asked him to pick blackberries for

a shortcake for supper. He snakeproofed himself and went over to the slope where the blackberries grow. I could hear him grumbling about the thorns. Soon he returned, somewhat scratched and with the berry pan only half full, a panicky look in his eyes. "Is this a tick?" he demanded, pulling up his shirt and pointing to one that had fastened itself to his side.

"Actually, it is," I replied, removing it.

"I don't think I like that job. I'll just catch up on some reading," he said, thumbing through the books on our shelves.

He refused to go outdoors at all and sat on the sofa reading *The Caine Mutiny*. After a few days he began to get bored and started tagging after Brian, who was rebuilding the engine on his 1948 pickup in the barn. Bruce had many observations to make on auto mechanics and no little advice to give. Eventually our son said he could help and gave him some rags and kerosene and showed him how to clean parts.

"How's it going?" I asked Bruce when he came into the house with a scowl on his face.

"Actually, I got grease on my clothing and . . . and . . . and on my body," he complained. I gave him some grease solvent and he daubed away at his body until it was suitably clean and then settled down by the window to watch the chickens scratching around outside for seeds and bugs.

The next day I suggested that he take charge of the chickens: He could feed and water them and collect the eggs. That pleased him.

"I know all about chickens," he told me.

I wasn't surprised.

"I visited a school once where they had chickens," he explained.

The feeding, watering, and egg gathering was uneventful at first, but I had not counted on the excitement that our number two rooster, Horny, could provide. Poor Horny has had to knuckle under to the leadership of the top rooster, Lewd, for a long time. Horny stores up his aggression until it bursts out occasionally in an attack on a non-chicken creature. Whenever he tries to prove that he is a better rooster than we are he is suitably trounced and retreats under the honeysuckle vine to stew about the unfairness of life.

Bruce was a new creature in Horny's world and he correctly sized him up as something that would run from him. Bruce came in the back door at top speed, scattering eggs. Eyes wide, he complained in a high-pitched voice, "One of those roosters chased me."

We all explained that yes, yes, the rooster had an inferiority complex, told of times when he had tried to attack us, and urged Bruce to go right back out with a big stick and chase Horny so that he would know that Bruce wasn't afraid of him. Reluctantly, armed with a piece of kindling, Bruce edged out the door where Horny was lurking.

The rooster backed off toward the honeysuckle, but was bewildered that he wasn't whacked on the head as usual. Instead, Bruce was ineffectually waving his piece of kindling and taunting, "Bad Horny. Get away from me." Horny wheeled and attacked. He managed to spur Bruce several times in the knee before Brian got out the back door. He grabbed

Horny by the legs, turned him upside down unceremoniously, shook him several times and tossed him over toward the honeysuckle where Lewd came rushing over to administer the final coup-de-coq that reminded Horny of his place in the general order of the universe.

Inside, Bruce hugged his wounded knee. I checked it and bathed the broken skin. He argued persuasively the need of a tetanus shot. It began to seem like not such a bad idea. He hadn't had one in several years and a rooster's spurs probably harbored tetanus. After all, the kid was away from home and how dreadful it would be to send him back with lockjaw. Brian drove him down to the hospital. Arm around Bruce's shoulder, he explained to the nurse on duty, "My man here has been gored by a chicken."

"No, no," exclaimed Bruce wildly. "A hawk, a hawk got me."

The nurse, Brian reported, looked amused as she administered the tetanus shot, but advised Bruce gravely, "Son, you're going to have to watch out for our Missouri chickens; they're a powerful breed."

For the next couple of days, Bruce rested his leg on the sofa, made considerable inroads on the aspirin bottle, and finished *The Caine Mutiny*. By the time he was done, his visit was nearly at an end.

We returned him to the airport in St. Louis. He walked with scarcely a limp toward the gate where his plane was to leave. He turned to us and with an urbane smile thanked us for the visit. "Actually, I've always wanted to read *The Caine Mutiny*," he said.

PRESS ON REGARDLESS

December 3, 1975

A while back, our twenty-year-old pickup truck, Press On Regardless, began to get choosy about the gears in which it wanted to travel. It decided that third gear was excessive and, when shifted into it, would balk and shift itself back into neutral.

For a time that was only a minor inconvenience because we use the truck mostly for hauling heavy loads around the farm and on rutty back roads where second gear is our preferred choice; but soon first gear went out, too.

My husband, Paul, decided that it was time to visit Jake's Junkyard to buy another transmission.

Jake is a balding, ruddy-faced man with a perennial two-day's-growth of beard. He lives in the center of his junkyard in a house furnished with auto leftovers and a freezer full of spare parts on his front stoop.

The morning when we limped over to the junkyard in second gear, Jake and two of his cronies were hunkered down in the dust behind an upended GMC pickup sharing a bottle of peppermint schnapps. Paul asked if Jake had a used transmission that would fit a '54 Chevy pickup. Jake did a quick mental inventory and was sorry that he didn't have one. But one of his friends knew an old boy on the other side of town who had one.

Everyone agreed that our truck wouldn't make it over there, so all of us—Jake, his two friends, the bottle of peppermint schnapps, Paul and I—climbed into what once must have been a Buick Special, although General Motors would have denied it.

The hood, of unknown make, was wired in place with electric fence wire and almost covered the old Lincoln engine. The back seat had been replaced with three plastic lawn chairs. I lowered myself into one, noticing that the roar of the engine indicated that Jake regarded tailpipes and mufflers as unnecessary frills. Nevertheless, Jake's car had a nice selection of gears available, and we were soon traveling at a good speed in one of the better gears on the highway toward the other side of town when the car shuddered alarmingly and lurched to one side. Jake eased it over to the shoulder before a screech of metal brought it to a full, if lopsided, stop.

I disentangled myself from a collapsed lawn chair and climbed out of the car to see the left rear wheel careen to a stop at the bottom of the roadside ditch. Jake's two friends were laughing and clapping him on the back. "You old fool," one sputtered. "You coulda killed us all. I told you them two lug nuts wouldn't hold."

Lug nuts, it appeared, are the fasteners that hold wheels to cars. Five on each wheel are the requisite and usual number, but the last time Jake had added new wheels to this car, he had lost one set. Making do, in the usual Ozark fashion, he had taken one from each of the two front wheels and used them to attach this last wheel. Jake and his friends, still chuckling, removed one lug nut from the right rear wheel and reattached the errant wheel.

I lapsed into catatonic rigidity for the rest of the drive, my knuckles turning white gripping the arm rests on the lawn chair. I visualized the wheels beneath us spinning looser and looser as we sped on—but hardly anything more fell off the car.

When we got to the old boy's place he had just sold his transmission, but he sent us on to a friend of his who had a junked truck and possibly a working transmission. That day we must have visited everyone in a twenty-mile radius of town who had ever owned a Chevrolet.

Jake and his friends didn't seem to worry about the looseness of the Buick's wheels. Nor did they concern themselves about the possible loss of junk-yard customers or even the lack of lunch. Apparently crazed by peppermint schnapps, their friendly and only concern was that we didn't have a working transmission. At the end of the afternoon we did find one and I was quite willing to pay the twenty dollars that the man wanted for it, but Jake patiently argued the price down, threatening, to my horror, to drive one hundred miles to a junkyard in Springfield, Missouri, before he would let his friends pay a penny more than fifteen dollars for it.

"No, no," I blurted out in a shrill voice. "We'll take it, won't we?" I appealed to Paul to help stop this nightmarish quest. Jake scowled at me and continued haggling. Men in the Ozarks are almost southern in their courtliness toward women, but they do not brook interference from women in important matters relating to dogs, guns, or auto mechanics. At last, to my immense relief, the man agreed to take fifteen dollars for it, and with the transmission nestled greasily at my feet, we returned to Jake's Junkyard.

I climbed into our truck, grateful that its wheels were buckled on securely, while Paul loaded the transmission into the back.

"That wife of yours is OK," I heard Jake say to Paul, "but a mite jumpy." He paused, his face puckered in concentration, searching for the right words. "A woman," he said gravely, "needs a lot of tuning up before she handles easy."

Paul smirked meanly all the way home.

GREEN WOOD AND HAM

January 3, 1976

"In a regular house," my friend said petulantly, "you turn a little knob and more heat comes out."

My friend, who professes a great love for country living and grows herbs on her windowsill in the city, had been house-sitting and taking care of our animals for four days while Paul and I moved one hundred hives of bees from northern Missouri to our farm in the southern part of the state.

She had never tended a wood-burning stove before, and she had been cold. The stove smoked, she reported. She couldn't figure out how to close the door. The fire wouldn't burn. Sometimes she got a bit of a flicker going by evening, but then it would go out overnight. She hadn't had time to paint any of the pots she'd brought with her and the only nature she'd communed with was a stick of firewood.

"But this is a regular house in the Ozarks," I protested. "And just about everyone has a wood stove here."

"I mean," she retorted, "a regular house in a real part of the country."

My arms ached from lifting thirteen thousand pounds of bees and honey and I was groggy from the long drive in the rented truck. Having been consigned to unregularity in an unreal land, all I could think to do was to build up the fire and go to bed.

The next day, apparently having made a mental note to cancel her subscription to *Mother Earth News*, my friend returned to the city, her thermostat, and her oil bills.

Our good old heating stove is black and has chrome trim. It stands in the middle of the living room floor with a demented grin on its cast-iron face. When we burn seasoned wood, it heats our four-room house efficiently. Even in the coldest part of the winter we can bank the fire at night, close the damper, and have a good bed of coals left in the morning.

But it is an old and honored tradition in our family to run out of seasoned firewood in January, and this year is no exception. From January until spring we burn green wood that gives off a tiny glow of heat around the stove. During these months we huddle around it. The beagle, a summer creature if I ever saw one, presses himself so close to the stove that his coat is singed curly.

We don't plan it that way, of course. The theory is that we will spend a week each spring out in the woodlot cutting enough wood for the following winter. Paul uses a chain saw, which is too heavy for me, to fell the trees and cut them into stove-length pieces.

I split them and stack the wood to season for the following winter.

Brian taught me to split wood a few years ago when Paul was recuperating from a concussion sustained when trying to lift the main barn beam with his head. Brian cut down several trees, but didn't have enough time to split the wood before he went back east, so he gave me a short course in wood splitting. Upend a log, drive in the wedge, stand back and hit the wedge with the maul.

"Give 'em no quarter," he advised, addressing himself to a particularly knotty and selfish log. And no quarter has been given in the years since. Actually I quite enjoy splitting logs; it satisfies a rage, brought on, no doubt, by spending too much of my time neatening up things—a row of vegetables, a room in the house, a hive of bees.

It is really rather pleasant work and Paul and I both enjoy it. Our plan is good, but the execution of it is shoddy. We spend a few days in the woodlot each spring and then queen bees start arriving, or the lettuce must be planted. Spring slips into summer and, grasshoppers that we are, we forget that winter will come again.

It's no excuse, of course, but most of the people I know never have enough wood for winter, either. We have one friend who is a woodcutter by trade. All year long he is out in the woods cutting poles for the post mill, oak logs for the charcoal factory, or firewood for people in town. His wife confessed to me that they never have more than a day's supply of wood—all of it green. She is thinking about buying a gas heater to keep from freezing to death this winter.

The only folks that I know who always have enough firewood are retired farmers who have moved into town and buy their wood, and people who work full time in offices. The latter are terrible bores on the Zen of woodpile management and, without fail, observe gravely that it was Thoreau who said wood warms twice: once when you cut it and again when it is on the fire. They regard woodcutting as a healthy outdoor weekend hobby. Their enthusiasm, though laudable, is hard to match when you've spent the week pouring concrete or putting up fences.

Any implied criticism is sour grapes, of course. Here it is January and I covet their woodpiles and admire the way they have their lives organized. Move over Beagle; I want to get warm.

WHAT'S GOING ON
IN THE GALLERIES

———

March 22, 1976

I read in the newspaper the other day that the Tate Gallery in London has paid twelve thousand dollars for a minimalist sculpture by Carl Andre. It's a pile of bricks, two bricks high, six bricks across, and ten long. Minimalists try to simplify and reduce art to the basics. The pile of bricks is supposedly relaxing, pleasant, and peaceful, but a number of people are wrathy about the twelve-thousand-dollar price tag and think that the Tate should have spent its money on something else.

I might have sided with those critics before we poured our concrete barn floor and got to know solid construction materials, but now I think that they are wrong. I have been heard to speak disparagingly of concrete construction and calumniously of some of the nation's noblest skyscrapers. No more. Now I take visitors out to the barn to admire the floor, its pervasive smoothness, its eye-catching gray color, its sturdy utility. They are polite about it, but I can tell right away that they are not truly moved by the floor and probably the passive viewer can never really appreciate its merit.

When we first looked at our farm with a real estate salesman, he gestured despairingly at the barn and said, "Of course, you'll want to tear down that old thing."

Of course we didn't.

The roof, made of old V-crimp metal sheets, was tied down with electric fence wire, but still flapped dangerously in windstorms. The beams were rotten as were the sills and studs. Much of the siding had been pried off for other building purposes. The barn was airy, so to speak. The floor was a well-trampled mixture of old crankcase oil, finely powdered mule manure, clay, and stone. But we needed a place for Paul to set up his tools for other construction and work on machinery, so it seemed more expedient to fix up the barn in a bootstrap sort of arrangement rather than tear it down.

Besides, secretly, I thought it was pretty.

In between other urgent jobs we started rebuilding the barn. We repaired the roof, replaced the beams, sills, and studs, and added new sheathing to keep out the wind and rain. It was less airy, but the floor was still the same damp surface, and Paul cursed foully every time he had to lie down on it to crawl under a piece of machinery. We began to think seriously about pouring a concrete floor.

We discovered that the entire floor area would have to be excavated at least four inches before we could haul in gravel for a base for the concrete. We started one morning, with goodwill, to dig it out with a pair of shovels. Soon we switched to pickaxes to break through the compacted surface. At the end of several hours we had excavated only a tiny area back in a gloomy corner of the barn. I was discouraged. My muscles ached. I suggested we go swimming, but we kept at our labors all day.

That evening I wearily drew a bath and soaked sullenly in the hot water thinking about being forty years old and just starting to develop my pickaxe skills. By the time I was done bathing, I had devised a splendid scheme whereby we would simply grade the present barn floor a little and whitewash it. Paul, a practical man, patiently explained to me the chemical difference between mule manure and concrete. We would continue. And we did, slowly, for several days until my nephew paid us a surprise visit one evening.

He was driving west from Pennsylvania with a couple of friends, seeking new horizons and a little excitement. The boys were enchanted with life on a real farm and said "far out" ever so many times. I cunningly explained the theory of bread labor, and the next morning issued them picks and shovels. They set to work on the barn floor while Paul and I retreated to the house for a cup of tea and rest for our tired backs. With our work force thus increased, we were able to get the floor excavated in just two more days. My nephew and his friends left quickly lest we think of any new entertainment.

Paul and I hauled gravel up from the river and spread it on the barn floor.

Pouring the concrete was slow work for the two of us. I could mix the stuff—gravel, sand, cement, and water—keep the mixture smooth, and dump it into a wheelbarrow, but I hadn't the strength to wheel it into the barn, nor the skill to smooth it. So whenever I had a load ready, Paul would stop troweling, wheel it into the barn and dump it. We would both spread it and I would mix another load while he troweled the surface smooth. At the end of forty-five minutes, we would stop and clean up the tools while he finished the surface of the section that would have started to set by then. We finished the barn shop floor, piece by slow piece in that fashion.

Brian came for a visit and volunteered to help us do the big center section of the barn floor. However, he and Paul were so busy working on Brian's '48 pickup to get it in proper shape to drive back to Boston that it wasn't until the last day of his visit that we had time to work on the barn floor. It was afternoon before we climbed into our cement-encrusted clothes and started up the cement mixer. I mixed, as before, but Brian trundled the heavy wheelbarrow into the barn, dumped it, and helped Paul spread the concrete. The work went much faster, but the increased pace was grueling.

The afternoon shadows lengthened and the sun went down. We strung up festoons of lights on ladders and continued working. My arms began to ache from hoisting the heavy buckets of sand, gravel and cement, and dumping them into the mixer, so Brian began lifting them for me. Conversation lagged, but

we doggedly kept mixing, pouring and leveling concrete. The sky was just beginning to lighten in the east
when we finished our last load. All three of us were
covered from head to toe with a thin layer of concrete
and we were powdered with cement dust.

The two men rinsed off the equipment and gal-
lantly allowed me the first bath. While they were
bathing, I fixed breakfast and began fretting about
Brian driving back to Boston. He came into the
kitchen, refreshed and unmarked by the night's labor,
and I began fussing at him, pointing out all the reasons
he should stay another day and get some sleep.

"Pish, and tush, woman, pish and tush," he said,
grinning and putting his arm around my shoulder. My
mothering always amuses him.

I laughed and looked up at him and remembered
the day I first noticed that he was taller than me and
knew that I could no longer tell him to go brush his
teeth.

After breakfast he packed his pickup and drove
eastward to a less strenuous life.

Paul and I, hand in hand, walked over to the barn
to admire our floor. There it lay, peaceful, as the
minimalists say. Its yellowishness was drying patchily
to a light gray, a handsome color. It was smooth and
beautiful, strong and serviceable, the testimony to
sixteen hours of backbreaking work. There it lay, a
veritable piece of sculpture.

I'm sorry, Tate Gallery people, but twelve thousand dollars won't buy that barn floor. Of course, if

you want to come up with an offer that would more nearly reflect its value, we might be willing to discuss it. If you want to talk it over, you'll find us out in the barn almost any afternoon.

FARLEY, THE CHICKEN
BABYSITTER

April 2, 1976

I've been recovering from a bout with the flu and haven't felt quite like myself. Indeed, I've felt rather like someone who'd been given vague directions on how to play me in a high school play and then muffed the part. Under the circumstances, about all I've felt capable of doing is watching the clutch of baby chicks that we are brooding under an electric light in a pasteboard box in the living room.

I am able to do this because there are only twelve of them; if there were twenty-four, I couldn't handle it. And even at that, I've been helped by Farley, our Irish setter who is a chicken expert. He watches them more than I do and does it better, but then, he doesn't have the flu.

In addition to the big red dog face that hangs down into the chicks' box, they have a blue plaid sky—an old bedspread that we pull over them at night. If anyone in the house sneezes, it sends them scurrying, peeping worriedly for a corner of their box.

Sneezes, the blue plaid sky, and the underside of a dog face are the only changing elements in their universe, which is otherwise made up of a round of eating, drinking, sleeping, and taking dust baths in their sawdust litter. A limited life, but they are thriving on it.

The reason that we are brooding these chicks in the living room is that the elder hens, out in the coop, can't handle it. They are hybrid Leghorns and there is no room in their tiny brains for anything but laying eggs. Broodiness has been almost bred out of them. A while back we did have one hen who went broody in a dreamy, disconnected sort of way. Fluffing out her tail, she retreated to a nest in the hen house where she sat on a clutch of eggs with a faraway look in her eye for several days.

Then she took to leaving the nest for longer and longer periods each day, allowing the eggs to become unconscionably cold; when she would return she would rearrange them in a fit of housewifeliness, usually rolling one or two right out of the nest where they would break. After a week, she had become so careless with her eggs that she had only one left. She finally gave it up as a bad job, apparently bored to distraction with motherhood, and returned to the routine of scratching under the honeysuckle bush, bug chasing, and professional egg laying with as much relief as a suburban matron who has just put the kids in nursery school and gone back to work in the city.

It is possible to purchase twenty-week-old pullets—ones that are just starting to lay—from our hatchery, but they come debeaked. Commercial egg farmers confine their chickens to tiny cages where the hens go stark raving mad and will peck and hurt each other unless their beaks are cut off. I won't have such deformed creatures on our farm, so we buy them a day old and raise them, under Farley's supervision, until they are ready to lay.

After they are feathered out, we put them with the rest of the flock. In the months between feathering and laying, they grow through a giddy, girlish phase. Incredibly light birds, they flutter when they run, soar for the fun of it, sometimes to the top of the house, and shriek and gabble excitedly as they pretend to be terrified by a falling leaf. Chicken Little must have been an adolescent pullet.

At about five months they grow more sedate and begin to lay. They never become blasé about being able to lay an egg, however, and I admire them for it. The hens and I all tend to regard what happens out there in the nest as the Miracle of the Egg. When she has laid her egg, a hen starts up with a guttural cackle and leaps down from the nest, celebrating excitedly "Cut-cut-cadawket, I did it. I did it," sometimes for ten or fifteen minutes at a stretch. Several dozen hens carrying on like this each day makes for a very lively barnyard.

At the moment, the chicks in the box in the living room are trying to figure out how to roost. They have a tiny, two-inch-high roost to practice on. They get up on it, teeter to attain their balance, and then can't quite think what to do with their heads, which they let dangle down heavily. I find it much easier to watch them when they are all lined up on the roost like that; with my head in the shape it is, they make me dizzy when they run around. But Farley is nervous when they all stop moving and go to sleep; he whines worriedly when they do that.

And, after all, he is the more responsible and less feverish chick watcher of us. I suspect that he can tell them apart. He's watched with interest as every feather has grown through the downy yellow fuzz on their stubby wings. At least I'm doing a better job watching them than those old hens outdoors would do. They would lose them right away, I know.

LIVING WITH BUGS

April 19, 1976

Out here in the country, where weather and the changing seasons are important, everyone has his own signs that tell when spring weather has arrived. To some it may be that first taste of rhubarb, or the dogwood blossoms in the woods, or even the sound of peepers out in the pond.

Those are all good spring signs, to be sure, but I never really think that weather has turned fair for good until the camel crickets start gnawing through the wallpaper at the head of our bed at night.

Camel crickets are blond, humpbacked insects with striped legs and they have none of their cousins' endearing habit of chirping cheerfully around the hearth. Camel crickets hang out in damp places (such as our walls) and then come out at night to try to find an open sack of dog food or crumbs in the corners. They are a nuisance, but do no real harm. They are rather handsome insects when you look at them the right way. However, I'm a jumpy person and when one crawls out of the wallpaper and across my arm at night, I am completely unnerved. Sleep is impossible, and I give myself over to listening for camel cricket noises and fretting about the spinach that never came up in the garden this year.

There is, of course, something basically unsound about our house or we wouldn't have it filled with camel crickets and swarming termites, another sure sign of spring. The house was built and added to, lovingly but without foresight, on the bare ground by generations of casual Ozark carpenters. Someday we're going to have to do something about it. Paul and I earnestly discuss building a stone house each spring on the day that the termites swarm out of the main beams, but we operate on a crisis basis around here and the termites swarm only one day and the camel crickets disappear of their own accord in June, so we'll probably live in this house until it falls down around our shoulders.

The worst of the springtime crawlers, however, are not even insects, but mites. The ticks and chiggers are around most of the year, but don't rate as nuisances except in the spring and summer just when we have lots of outdoor work to do in our beekeeping business. Most of our bee outyards are at the edges of woods on good bottom land farms where the clover thrives. Long grasses, low shrubs, and trees are what ticks like best. And they hang there, ready to grab on to us as we go to work with bees.

The ticks are loathsome creatures, fastening on to warm-blooded animals with their mouths and burrowing in for feed. Even our dogs dislike them, and shake their heads and snap at them distastefully when they come across an engorged tick that has dropped off and is creeping along the ground.

About the only good thing I can think to say about Ozark ticks is that they aren't so bad as California ticks. We lived in California for a time, and the ticks there are more numerous and harder to remove. The only way to get them off is to unscrew them counterclockwise. Even then the mouth parts occasionally break off and leave a festering sore that takes weeks to heal.

The grand finale of the tick season in the Ozarks comes in late August and early September when the tiny seed ticks hatch out of eggs. They lurk where they have hatched, waiting to catch a ride on a bare arm or leg that brushes up against them. It is impossible to scrape or wash them off, so when we go out in the woods at that time of year we carry a roll of masking tape. A bit of tape, daubed sticky side down, will trap them and pull them off before they can spread itchily all over the body.

At least ticks can be seen, but chiggers are nearly invisible. They are the larval stage of a mite that hatches out of small brown eggs laid in moist soil. They creep up the legs until they come to a place where clothing binds and there they settle to chew, injecting a fluid that produces the most ferociously itchy bites I've ever known.

A dusting of sulphur about the boot tops helps keep them down, but a friend of mine tells me that the only sure way to keep from getting chigger bites is not to wear any clothes at all. Presumably the chiggers walk right up a naked body and, not finding any tight clothing, just walk right down the other side. That solution to the problem has a certain sweet reasonableness, but inasmuch as I've never been able to talk myself into plunging naked into the brambles when I go to pick blackberries, I can't report on its effectiveness.

If left to their own devices, creatures interrelate quite nicely, each working away in his own niche, and cutting down the other fellows when they get too many. I can appreciate the camel cricket as a scavenger and admire the termite's habit of reducing everything to basic elements. Even the chigger has its place. Those biting larvae grow up to be adults that are predators on insects and insect eggs.

As a warm-blooded creature, it's a bit hard for me to work up much liking for ticks or to understand why the world wouldn't be a better place without them. But our Ozark hills and woods and rivers are lovely beyond compare, and perhaps the ticks help keep the tourists down. If the woods weren't full of ticks, they'd be full of people. Then there would be less space for the wild dogwood and the redbud, the serviceberry, and the sumac. The wild blackberries and mushrooms would be trampled underfoot and the thickets that the wild turkeys haunt would be cleared away.

Everything considered, I guess I'll take the ticks.

EGG HUSTLING

———

April 27, 1976

I'm ashamed to say that I never gave the farm-surplus problem much thought until my husband and I moved to our ninety-acre farm in the Ozarks. We discovered that farming on even that small a scale could produce a surplus that made us believe we had taken quarters under the business end of cornucopia.

Our surplus began modestly enough with the arrival of twenty-four fluffy, peeping, day-old pullets. There were twenty-four instead of the twelve that we thought we needed because we assumed, after reading pamphlets and textbooks on poultry rearing, that at least half of them would die from diseases with terrible names such as coccidiosis. But they didn't and within five months they were presenting us with twenty eggs a day.

After a couple of weeks we had eaten all the omelets and custard that we could stomach. Our friends all had chickens that were laying and didn't want any extra eggs. We couldn't nail up a sign in front of our house that said EGGS FOR SALE and expect to get any results because we live at the dead end of a two-mile dirt road.

We had noticed that some farmers brought fruit and vegetables into town on Saturday mornings and sold them from the backs of their pickups, which they parked near the Saturday morning auction. I had also noticed modish women selling cookies and pies for worthy causes in front of a boarded-up store on the main street. So one Saturday morning when we couldn't squeeze another egg in the refrigerator, we packed twelve dozen eggs in cartons into a big box and drove into town.

Paul had to stop at the hardware store to buy some carriage bolts, so while he did that I considered what to do with the eggs. It seemed a trifle uppity to take the box of eggs—the product of a mistake, as it were—over to where the real farmers sold their vegetables and fruit. Perhaps if I took them to the place where the bake sales were held, someone, in a spirit of charity, would buy eggs. I unloaded the egg box nervously, and trying desperately to look casual, unpacked it in front of the boarded-up store. Nonchalantly, I turned around to tape up a hand-lettered sign that I had made saying that yes, these were eggs and that they were for sale for ever so modest a price. When I turned back around, I was surrounded by a ring of people snatching up cartons of eggs. Within three minutes they were all gone. People really wanted to buy eggs! Paul sauntered down the sidewalk from the hardware store, grinning with amusement at the startled look on my face and the fistful of small change dribbling through my fingers.

"Pretty good, Sue," he said laughing and hugging me around the shoulders. "I guess we really are farmers."

After that we took eggs into town every Saturday morning to sell. The strawberries ripened and I packed them in little cartons, took them along with the eggs, and arranged them in rows on the sidewalk and sold them, too. Later in the summer, I sold tomatoes and corn the same way.

When Brian came here for a visit from Boston he was appalled to find his mother hustling eggs on the street corner. Life is more formal and commerce more regulated in Boston.

"Don't you need a meddler's license to do this?" he asked wryly the first Saturday morning that he was home as he lifted the big box of eggs out of the pickup for me. True, I sometimes wondered if some bureaucratic procedure wasn't being violated by hawking our agricultural surplus on the street. It seemed so direct, so simple and so logical that it must be irregular in some way. But when any one of the three town policemen would cruise by, he would wave in a friendly way. The deputy sheriff occasionally walked past on his way to the barbershop for his Saturday morning haircut and he would tip his hat politely. So I guess that dealing eggs and produce on the sidewalk isn't illegal, but it must be outrageous, because the following year, the bank, in a fit of civic service, turned over the last row of its parking lot to local gardeners for a farmer's market.

Now we drive into town on Saturday morning and park behind the bank, put down the tailgate, and hang up the portable scales on a crossbar over the stock rack. We arrange the tomatoes and sweet corn in baskets, heap the pumpkins on the pavement at the side of the truck, put the eggs out on the tailgate, and stack the honey from our hives on cartons in back of the eggs.

There is a flurry of selling to a little knot of customers who have been waiting for us to unpack. Then we settle down on portable stools and wait for other buyers. A woman comes up and peers suspiciously at the eggs; her eyes narrow as she looks at me.

"What kind of eggs are these?" she asks severely.

I had promised myself that the next person who asked that question would get a smart answer: "Alligator eggs, nice fresh alligator eggs," or perhaps, "This week, lady, we've got the special assortment—raspberry, pineapple, and chocolate with cherry centers." But instead I just mumbled, "Ah . . . er . . . you know . . . chicken eggs," and she walks off, sniffing disapprovingly. I don't know why.

The next few customers buy all the eggs, some tomatoes, and honey.

A stoop-shouldered old man in a cardigan sweater shuffles up to me and in a soft voice asks, "Okry? Got any okry?" I shake my head and say that I'm sorry, but I didn't grow any okra this year. He asks every week.

A couple of hippies wander up to the truck. "Hey man, those tomatoes are like the sun," one exclaims, holding a tomato aloft. We all appreciate the tomato a whole lot and then he puts it down, gently, and ambles away.

Other customers buy our produce and chat about

the weather, the general health of gardens this year, things of consequence to country folk. The woman who had asked me to pot her some herbs comes by to pick them up. The banker comes out of his office and beams happily as he watches someone buy all of our pumpkins.

In an hour or so the truck is empty. Our surplus is gone and we have a pocketful of money. Redistribution of food. Hum of commerce. Heady stuff. Maybe it's not a commodity exchange, but it'll do, it'll do.

NOT REPUBLICANS

May 13, 1976

I've been musing about goat sheds lately and I hate it.

Don't think for a minute that I don't know what's happening to me. I do. I have an aunt who went to seed over animals. She adopted stray creatures of every sort, made a general nuisance of herself by sneaking around at night untying neighborhood dogs that she thought shouldn't be tethered, and then lost almost all of her friends by reporting them to the Society for the Prevention of Cruelty to Animals for alleged unkindness to animals.

Now in her old age she is an unsought campaigner for the Democratic Party. During election times, she lurks in supermarkets to buttonhole Republicans and remind them pointedly about whose fault it is that food prices are going up. You can always tell Republicans, she says. They are buying whipping cream.

So far, I haven't felt any urge to skulk around the dairy counter in the grocery, but I notice that I am growing increasingly dotty over animals.

Aside from our thirty million bees scattered around the countryside and the twenty-eight chickens, one of whom has hurt her leg and is living in the bathtub, we are on intimate terms with three dogs and two cats. They are all neurotic from being part of a human pack, although they refuse to have it any other way.

Durrell, our oldest dog, is a polite and well-behaved Irish setter. He is a gentleman and a scholar of our moods. He worries a lot. He is the only dog I have ever known cursed with a superego. The vet says he has hypoglycemia, so in these latter years he has developed a mania about food—its possibility or presence. He knows that we object to his panting in excitement while cadging leftovers at the dinner table, and so by God knows what effort he keeps his mouth closed. His cheeks rhythmically billow in and out with the effort, but he keeps his teeth tightly clenched.

The other Irish setter, Farley, is quite a different dog. Raffish, independent, and moody, he puts up with the quiet life on the farm for a few weeks at a time and then takes off for town, about seven miles distant, to indulge in his low tastes, rooting around in the garbage at the drive-in and hanging out at service stations until we come for him.

At home, the chickens are his responsibility. He keeps them herded in a tight little knot around the chicken-coop door. We have encouraged him in this work because hawks have killed several chickens that have strayed too far when Farley was in town. Chickens are an unruly lot, and when Farley doesn't keep a close eye on them, they stray out to the compost heap and then to the field and beyond. When he spots them out there, Farley rushes out, running the last few feet with his belly close to the ground and then he halts near them, crouched, tense, glaring. The chickens panic and run clucking nervously back to the safety of the coop, except for a few stragglers who are so busy scratching and exchanging gossip about a particularly fine beetle that they don't notice him.

Farley ignores all but the farthest chicken and concentrates his almost electric powers on her. Soon she becomes aware of him, as do the others, and they all lose their nerve and appetite and run squawking and flapping back home, victims of the whammy.

I was a pushover for the last dog we took in. We found him, a hairless, starved, mangy, and wormy rat-sized infant out in the road leading up to our place. Someone had probably tossed out an unwanted litter of hounds, and he was the survivor. Paul and I got out of the pickup to look at him, wondering aloud how he got there and what was to be done with him. He looked at me, sensing that I was a soft touch, and weakly wagged his tail. "Why are we standing here?" Paul asked, wearily watching me croon at the pup. "You know what we are going to do with him." So I scooped him up, all loathsome and dear, and took him home to start dosing and bathing him. Today, Andy, probably a cross between a beagle and a foxhound, is spoiled beyond belief, a thirty-five-pound lap dog who believes that it is his inalienable right to share the brown leather chair with anyone reading the newspaper there. I guess he is a rabbit dog—at least he enjoys spending the afternoon tracking and baying—but I notice hunters' smiles turn sour when they see him crawl up in my lap to be cuddled.

The cats thread their ways through this dog-dominated household. Margaret is a sour-tempered old bat who spends her time curled up on the foot-stool, meditating on the wrongs done her. She regards herself as the Primary Creature in the house, certainly not a cat. She loathes all the others, whom she regards as interlopers and hates them most particularly at meal-time. In deference to her age and strong opinions, I feed her in a room apart from her daughter Tertia.

Tertia is a beautiful tortoiseshell cat, an adept hunter who once killed a copperhead that was coiled up by our back door. Her particular neurosis is doors. I don't know what her fear is based on, but sometimes it takes her five minutes to go in or out an open door. She makes tentative little creeps toward the doorway, panics and retreats, screws up her courage, inches forward and is defeated by fear again.

Paul grows impatient and boots her out the door, but I keep hoping she'll overcome her problems, so I wait for her with the door open. A month ago, Tertia's worst fears materialized. We had been gone a couple of hours in town doing errands. We came home, had lunch, and idled about a bit. Then I opened the back door to go out. There, squeezed very thinly between door and screen door was Tertia, the prisoner of an unnoticed attempt to go in or out earlier in the day. Her eyes were wide but she seemed resigned to the knowledge that the door, in its attempt to kill her had just scored a point—a point that she had known all along it would make. She walked out calmly, waving her tail and took a dainty sip from the chickens' watering pan.

For a long time I have been fighting the impulse to add to our animal population. All our back-to-the-land friends keep urging us to get a goat. They tell us that these animals are intelligent and endearing. I point out that the twice-a-day milking schedule is impossibly confining, that goats are destructive. But a few months ago a friend of mine taught me how to milk a goat. Before I quite realized it, I was sitting there, my head against the goat's warm side, milking and thinking what a fine addition a goat would make to our farm and how good it would be to have our own fresh milk.

My friend has just invited me over to see some new kids. Dear Apollo, protect me, I know I don't want a goat, yet I fear that I'm slipping.

KARMA KASTLES

June 3, 1976

For four long years I worked in the library of an Ivy
League university and about the only excitement I can
remember took place the day the Assistant Librarian,
a rumpled, inept fellow, flushed a book thief from the
stacks, chased him through the lobby, and pinned him
in the revolving door, only because his own arm was
wedged in the door, too.

The campus police came, took the miscreant into
custody and freed the Assistant Librarian. We talked
about it during coffee breaks for weeks.

Life on an Ozark farm is different. Take any day.
Take yesterday, for instance.

Paul and I had just bought a big 1951 Chevy
three-quarter-ton flatbed truck for hauling beehives
in our expanding honey business. We knew that it
lacked brakes and that its ignition system was a little
sketchy, so we took a chain and homemade tow bar
when we went to get it in our pickup. The big truck
wouldn't start, so we fastened the chain to the front of

it and hitched it to the pickup. I drove the pickup and watched Paul in the rearview mirror giving me cryptic hand signals while he steered the big truck.

The transmission on our pickup had been giving us some trouble and I could feel the strain as it towed the heavy load up the hills on our lane. We were almost home, within one hundred yards of our driveway, when we came to the steepest hill of all. I floored the accelerator, the wheels spun briefly, and we started slowly up the hill. Then there was the sharp sound of steel snapping, a clatter, and no more power. Something essential had sheared loose. We tried rolling both trucks back down the hill in tandem, but that was impossible, so Paul loosened the tow chain. The big truck started rolling, Paul ran after it, jumped in and regained the steering, but not before it had careened into the ditch at the side of the lane. I let the pickup roll backwards and brought it to a stop next to the big truck.

Just a regular Ozark farm morning.

We trudged up the hill, Paul muttering about General Motors, to get the tractor to pull both trucks up to the barn. Paul climbed up on the tractor seat and tried to start it. The battery was dead. He climbed back down and we stood there, bleakly, thinking what to do next when we heard the sound of a motorcycle coming up the driveway. Sandor, a large furry fellow, was driving it, and his wife, Fourth True Star, was holding on to him, a diaphanous dress and rattlesnake headband blowing out behind her.

Sandor and Fourth True Star are a part of the

growing band of hippies that are settling in the Ozarks. They garden with fervor, straighten used nails, and recycle old barn lumber, living so cheaply that it astonishes even the native Ozarkers who are past masters at getting by. They are outrageously colorful.

"I have come to this peaceful space for a time," Fourth True Star said brightly as she jumped off the motorcycle. "I wish to free myself from karmakassles."

"Karma castles?" I inquired. It sounded like a place to buy burgers.

"Karmic *hassles*," she repeated with just a faint edge of irritation in her voice.

"Swell. That's just swell," I said, doubtful that ours was a peaceful space at the moment.

Sandor looked glum as he unstrapped her astrology books from the motorcycle. "We are all children," he said irrelevantly, and drove off, threading his way between the disabled trucks at the bottom of the hill.

I suggested that Fourth True Star make herself at home while we tried to get the various machines running. We still had one vehicle that would go. The last time Brian had visited us, he left his 1948 pickup behind. It suffered from some minor mechanical ills which prevented him from driving it back to the East Coast, but Paul thought we could use it to tow the tractor to get it started. We hitched the tow chain to the pickup's bumper and the tractor. Paul climbed up on the tractor and I got into the pickup and cautiously stepped on the accelerator, again watching Paul's mysterious hand signals. The truck lurched forward and was free. I had pulled off its back bumper. Paul's temper was not getting any better and I burst into tears.

Just another Ozark farm day moving along as usual.

Patiently, Paul soothed me, gave me a brief rundown on the meaning of the hand signals, and fastened the tow chain onto something secure under the pickup. This time, I was able to keep the truck running evenly, towed the tractor along, and soon its engine kicked on.

We drove the tractor down the hill at the end of the driveway and towed our pickup back up. We returned with the tractor and fastened the tow chain to the big three-quarter-ton truck while I was supposed to steer while Paul drove the tractor. He got on the tractor, accelerated, and the engine died and would not start again. Sometimes it is better to leave a man alone, so I tiptoed up the hill and busied myself cleaning out the chicken coop and adding a layer to the compost pile.

Fourth True Star came out to watch. "Sandor and I want to make a garden this year," she said. "We are both organic, of course, but I wish to go biodynamic and Sandor is not yet ready to make that commitment."

"What do you mean?" I asked.

"I honor the yarrow and wish to expose the carrot

seed to the light of the pure, new moon. It's putting a terrible strain on our relationship."

Sometimes the hip life is not easy.

Paul walked up the driveway, looking very grim. He had tried to start the tractor by letting it roll down the rutty road to the river, but couldn't get up enough speed to get the engine going. Now the tractor was at the edge of the river with rocks braking its wheels. He wanted me to help tow it up backwards with Brian's pickup. I was afraid to drive the truck up the road, so I volunteered to steer the tractor. The backwards steering was awkward and strange and I overcompensated for swing in the steering as the tractor swayed from one side of the road to the other. I panicked and screamed "Help!" so loudly that Paul heard it over the roar of the engine. He stopped the pickup, got out, and started laughing.

"We usually use hand signals," he reminded me.

"I'm scared. What do I do when the tractor tips over," I asked cravenly. He explained to me that it was impossible for the tractor to tip over. I didn't believe him for one minute, but agreed to try again. We reached the crest of the river road where the big three-quarter-ton truck was still resting idly in the ditch, turned the corner and continued on up the hill to get the tractor high enough for a rolling start. The steering wheel spun wildly in my hand and I steered into a tree.

Paul didn't really meet my eye as he got out of the pickup, but said, "It's okay. I think I can start it from here." He rolled the tractor down the hill. It started and he backed it into a place in front of the big truck. We hitched the chain to the truck and towed it up the hill over to the barn.

It had taken all day, but we had all of our vehicles around the barn, never mind that they didn't run. We walked across the barnyard to the house. Fourth True Star was in the kitchen. She had just made a peanut butter chiffon pie and wondered if we would like a piece with a cup of herb tea. It wasn't nearly as bad as it sounds.

"I have just been consulting your natal charts," she said. "This is not a good day for either of you to work with machinery."

"Far out," Paul said weakly.

Just your usual, ordinary day on a farm in the Ozarks.

AN UPPITY WOMAN

June 14, 1976

Ozark men are . . . well . . . not liberated. They rush
to open doors for women, offer to carry packages
weighing over ten pounds, and, apparently, were all
taught to address women as "ma'am" when they were
children and find the habit impossible to break as
adults. They believe that a woman's place is sitting
quietly on the passenger's side of the pickup waiting
for "her man."

She most emphatically should not get out and kick
tires or make a hole in the gravel with the toe of her
shoe and talk about dogs with the real people. A
woman may sometimes be spoken to concerning the
weather if it is unusual enough, but under no circumstances should she be looked in the eye. Whenever
possible it is best to pretend that she isn't there at all.

I have a friend whose husband is often away on
business. She reports that whenever men come over
to visit, they cautiously inquire if her husband is
home; if he's not, they refuse to even get out of their

pickups. Our insurance agent thinks I'm joking when I talk business with him. If I drive into town alone and try to get the gasoline tank filled, the man at the service station asks me severely, "Where's your husband?"—as though I had sneaked into town with a stack of dollar bills that I was going to fritter on gasoline without proper masculine authorization.

Now there are a few men around here like my favorite VW mechanic and the accountant, both of whom readily admit that women are human beings, possibly even capable of rational thought, but there are others like our, or I should say, Paul's friend, Troy.

The first time we met Troy, a young, spare, intense man with a blond pompadour, we were new in town and had gone into the store where he worked to open an account. I asked him several questions. He blushed and looked unwaveringly over my shoulder at my husband, Paul, and prefaced each answer with Paul's name to make it clear to whom he was speaking. We would see him from time to time and he was always hearty and friendly . . . to Paul. By that time I had discovered that Ozark people are polite to a fault and that he was not really being rude, but that since I was a woman, I simply didn't count.

One day in the spring, I bought a new garden tiller for too many dollars for me to be comfortable. I decided to go into the garden tilling business to help pay for it and put an ad in the local newspaper offering my services. One day when Paul and I were in town, Troy stopped us and asked Paul to till his garden for him.

"But it's Sue that's doing the tilling. Better ask her," Paul said, gesturing toward me, standing there all unnoticeable beside him.

Troy colored and replied, looking hard at Paul, "Well, Paul, I sure would appreciate it if you could get out to my place before next Wednesday and till my garden." Then, as he turned on his heel, he glanced briefly in my direction, murmured "Morning, ma'am," and fled.

A few days later we drove over to Troy's house. Paul helped me unload the heavy tiller from the pickup and then started to climb back into the truck to go do some errands. Troy burst from his house and grabbed Paul by the elbow. "I'll show you where I want tilled, Paul," he said, a little out of breath.

"Why don't you show Sue?" my husband asked.

"I want to show you, Paul," Troy said firmly, dragging my husband over to his garden spot. I tagged along behind, pushing the tiller. Troy pointed out all the garden boundaries to Paul, who, in turn, gravely pointed them out to me and then left, giving me a wink. I spent the next two hours tilling and then wheeled the machine out beside the road and sat down waiting for Paul to come back. When he drove up, Troy dashed out of the house and paid him. I sputtered all the way home, but Paul laughed and said that he'd see that I got a regular allowance out of my earnings.

One Sunday, later that summer, we were in front of our barn, rebuilding the engine of our pickup when we saw Troy drive by the end of our driveway and down the rutty road to the river in his new green pickup. He and a couple of friends who were with him waved. A little later the report of a .22-caliber rifle indicated that they had come out to the river for an afternoon of squirrel hunting.

After several hours, I looked up to see Troy walking up our driveway, carrying his gun. He was trailed by his two friends who were laughing and swinging the remains of several six-packs of beer by their plastic loops.

Troy was not laughing.

I was nearest to them, so I straightened up and called out a welcome.

Troy's friends stopped laughing.

Troy looked past my left ear at Paul who was bent over the engine and got right down to business.

"Stuck. Damn truck's stuck in a foot of gravel," he said.

During the course of the afternoon's shooting and drinking, a variety of claims and challenges had been exchanged concerning the manhood of Troy's truck. To deal with the situation, Troy had tried to drive his shiny new truck across the river and it was mired there. He and his friends needed a ride into town to get the wrecker.

Paul was right in the middle of a tricky piece of mechanics, but he didn't need my help for the moment, so I offered to drive the three men into town in our van. Troy's friends hopped into the back. I climbed into the driver's seat. That left Troy no choice. He sat down gingerly on the seat beside me, but put his gun between us lest I try anything funny.

One of our dogs, always keen for a ride, jumped in the open car door and sat down on the gun. I started the van and headed down the road for town.

"Nice weather for this time of year," I said, experimentally.

Troy stared straight ahead and clenched his teeth. His friends laughed nervously. The dog, seeking a more comfortable seat, eased himself over onto Troy's lap. Troy looked cramped.

"You don't have to put up with that dog on your lap," I said. "Push him off." Troy turned red. His brow furrowed and he concentrated very hard on a tiny spot directly in front of us on the road. The dog sighed luxuriously and we drove into town silently.

When we got to Troy's house, the two men in back leaped from the van and whispered "Thank you, ma'am," eyes to the ground.

I pulled the dog from Troy's lap and he climbed out stiffly and grabbed his gun. He pointed it straight up in the air and fired, yelling "W★H★O★O★O★P-★E★E!!" obviously delighted beyond measure that he was home safe. I hadn't molested him or even talked to him much.

I drove back to our place with the dog. He had jumped when the gun was shot off, but, on the whole, seemed less puzzled by events than I.

I had never dared to believe that Troy and I would become chums, but I had hoped that our shared ride to town might confer existence upon me. But we saw Troy in town a couple of days ago. I greeted him with a cheery "Hello."

Panic flickered across his face momentarily, but

51

then he grinned and clapped my husband on the shoulder and said, "Hi there, Paul. Where you been keeping yourself? Haven't seen you since that day you helped us out when the truck got stuck. I did appreciate that."

Living in the Ozarks is nice, but it sure does make a body invisible sometimes.

TIME MANAGEMENT AND PANSIES

July 26, 1976

When Paul and I moved to our farm in the Ozarks, I had the distinct impression that we were retiring. The people in our offices had given us both retirement parties and told us how lucky we were to be "getting out of the rat race."

The last time I commuted from the office on the interstate, I sighed with relief as I pulled up in our driveway and uncurled my fingers from the steering wheel. No more TV dinners, I promised myself. I was going to have time to cook. Life was going to be more leisurely.

There would be some work to do, but never on the long winter evenings when we would sit around the woodstove and make popcorn, or on the lazy summer afternoons when we would go swimming. One of the first purchases we made when we moved to our farm was a hammock to lie in and read light novels.

Alas, that is not the way it is at all. We're eating

packaged meals because we are too busy growing our own food to cook it. We spend our long winter evenings rebuilding the tractor engine and repairing apiary equipment. The hammock swings under the two pine trees, empty, weathering, although it is true that I tried it once last summer for half an hour to let the aspirin work on my headache after a particularly hectic afternoon working with the bees. Are these our golden retirement years?

I'm not too good at arithmetic, but according to the records I keep for our honey business, we spent thirty-four days last month working with bees. That is absurd, I know, but what is even more absurd, is that in our spare time that same month we did a lot of work in the garden and took care of several emergencies, including, but not limited to, repairing the water pump after it was knocked out in an electrical storm; transporting to the river six turtles that made their ways at various times into the perennial garden and were eating the strawberries; and installing new king pins in the pickup when it broke down on a day when the bees had decided to swarm.

We didn't lie in the hammock at all.

There's too much to do and something has to be eliminated. I've just decided to skip cooking and housework.

Our lives have developed an excessive quality since moving to the Ozarks. The pansies are an example. We have a small greenhouse where I start tomatoes, herbs, cabbages, and flowers for our garden and for sale. This year, I decided to grow some pansies to sell. Pansies are tricky and I spent a lot of time fussing with them to get them to germinate. I thinned them, encouraged them, and transplanted them. By the time they were ready, I couldn't bring myself to put them in plastic boxes and sell them, so we transplanted them to our big garden, where they line all the pathways and grow between the rows of vegetables.

They are very pretty, but they are very many. Pansies won't continue to bloom unless they are picked frequently and not allowed to go to seed, so I pick pansies

I pick pansies when I should be weeding the strawberries or hanging out the laundry. I pick pansies when I should be mulching the squash or nailing together new frames for honeycombs. I pick pansies when I should be cleaning the chicken coop or canning beans. Last night I picked a peach basket full of pansies and spent an hour arranging them in peanut butter jars, feeling harried all the time.

Paul thought it was funny to harvest pansies by the bushel, but I've been spinning a fantasy about hiring help. Paul could use a live-in mechanic. Farm work, it turns out, is 80 percent mending things, but I'll settle for a seven-year-old girl, one who would like to pick flowers and be very careful with them and arrange them in bouquets.

I want to lie in that hammock. I complain about it a lot.

"But," Paul says gently, "this is our busy season."

"You've been saying that for four years," I remind him.

The longer we live here, the more extravagant

grows my admiration for our Ozark neighbors. They cut their firewood on time. They plow their gardens when the soil is just right. They plant their potatoes on the correct date. Their houses are tidy and weeds never grow in their gardens. Their pickups run. And they still have time to sit down at the café in town and have a cup of coffee. They don't drum their fingers nervously on the counter, either.

It's true that they don't have bees, but I think that they have their priorities better in mind than we do, and they are smarter, too. They have enough sense not to grow pansies.

DAISY HAY

August 6, 1976

It's haying time down here in the Ozarks. The folks with smiles on their faces are those who got their hay cut, raked, baled, and stacked in between rainstorms. Those who don't look so happy got caught in showers with their hay down.

We make hay, preferably while the sun shines, out here on our farm, although I suppose our hay making has about as much to do with the real thing as the bucolic life Marie Antoinette played at in shepherdess costume at the Petit Trianon does to sheep ranching. Nevertheless, we do make hay of a sort. Because we don't feed any grass-eating animals, we don't really care if it rains on our hay. We need it for mulch for the two gardens, the orchard, and the compost piles that have insatiable appetites for organic materials.

One of our problems—an aesthetic one—never confronts agribusinessmen. We've limned and fertilized our small hay field and it gives us good orchard grass and clover hay, but not enough, so we have to go out in back of the barn and mow the daisy field. It makes pretty hay, but after walking in the moonlight in a shimmering field of daisies, it seems crass to cut daisies for hay. We are loathe to mow them and keep putting off our hay making.

Even after we have become severe with ourselves and cut all of our hay, there still is not enough and I have to use old newspapers for mulch between the rows of sweet corn. Truth forces me to report that the *New York Times* makes better mulch than the *St. Louis Post-Dispatch*. The *Times* is printed mostly in six-sheet sections that can be divided conveniently into halves that fit between the rows of corn, but the more numerous four-sheet sections of the *Post* don't really do the job when split in two and are somewhat prodigal as mulch when left entire.

But the reason that this isn't a real hay-making operation out here is that it is too much fun and I know from the talk I hear around the feed store that haying is serious business.

After we cut our hay with a mower strapped to the belly of our tractor, we rake it with an old-time dump rake hitched behind the tractor. Paul drives the tractor and I sit up on the seat between the two big rake wheels and operate the foot pedals to make the tines rake and then dump the hay in long windrows.

The view from the seat of the rake is fine. The wheels bump crazily over rocks and gullies as we rake. The seat is slightly loose and that gives the ride an ineffable quality—a sidewise wobble is added to the inherent bounce and forward motion. It is a ride for which even the most liberated woman needs a bra. It is a ride definitely worth a quarter at any amusement park on the Jersey shore.

The first time we cut hay, a few years back, we didn't have a rake. In my enthusiasm, inexperience, and naivete, I promised that if Paul would cut the hay, I would rake it by hand. After the second day in the hot sun trying to rake up a ten-acre field with a broom rake that had seen service only on a suburban lawn, my sweet, sunny temper was utterly spoiled.

We set out looking for a used hay rake to buy.

When an Ozarker wants to sell something that is too big or too heavy to take into town for the weekly auction, he simply drags it out on his front lawn, never mind the "for sale" sign. Eventually somebody comes along and asks how much he'd have to give to own it. The seller looks out at the horizon. A price is stated. The buyer speculates on the weather. A counter offer is made. The seller tells an entertaining story concerning that coon hound over yonder. Another go-around on price follows. The two seriously discuss the virtues of open drive shafts over closed ones. A deal is made.

We didn't understand that method of doing business when we first moved here and wasted a good deal of time looking for a used cement mixer to buy. But when, at last, a friend explained about all those things out in front yards, we could see that the countryside was fairly bristling with cement mixers for sale and quickly bought one. So when we started looking for a dump rake, we drove around on backroads and peered into yards.

The first rake that we found needed too much

repair work to make it usable. We found one farm-house that had two rakes out on the lawn. We asked about them, but the woman in the house said that her husband didn't want to sell them. "They remind us of Grandpaw," she said.

"Both of them?" Paul asked incredulously.

"Yep, both of them," she replied.

We drove away, picturing the maestro of hay makers who presumably hitched up his two rakes to a team and stood astride the two lead horses, lashing them to a gallop and shouting directions while two strapping sons manned the rakes' levers, raking and dumping frenziedly.

After a few more stops we found a rake that needed only minor repairs. The owner wanted an outrageous price for it, but we aren't very good hag-glers so we paid his price and hitched the rake to the back of our pickup and drove slowly home, the rake bouncing along behind us, totally out of control and squeaking alarmingly.

When we got it home, Paul repaired the rake, sanded off the rust, and painted it. The main part is bright aquamarine blue and the wheels are golden yellow. Oldtimers around here are fond of dump rakes and think that ours is a dandy except for the paint job which, they hold, is a mite garish.

A country neighbor and longtime farmer stopped by while we were raking a few days ago. The sun was low in the sky and we wanted to finish our hay making before dark. Our friend lounged against the side of his pickup watching us when Paul shifted the tractor to high speed and opened the throttle. We hurtled wildly over the daisy field, raking and dumping furiously with our colorful rake, the wheels bouncing me high in the seat. When we got back to the barn, our friend was doubled over laughing. He said he hadn't seen anything so entertaining since he watched a Charlie Chaplin film back in the twenties.

GREAT CORN MADNESS

August 20, 1976

Some years back when Paul and I found ourselves with a bad case of caffeine jitters, we swore off coffee and threw out our coffee pot. We quit cold turkey, going from a twelve-cup-a-day habit to nothing. We suffered withdrawal symptoms for two weeks: aching backs, heads, and legs, and an intense desire to sleep twenty hours out of the twenty-four. Afterward we found that having been so severely addicted, we were enormously sensitive to even a little caffeine and an occasional cup of coffee would give us a fantastic fifteen-cent high. The world would seem rosy, life a piece of cake, and all things possible.

A coffee high is to blame for what has become known locally as the Great Corn Madness, or Hubbell's Folly.

The groundwork was laid the summer before when we learned enough about living in the country and working our half-acre garden to take a pickup full of fruit, vegetables, eggs, and honey into town each morning to sell at the Farmer's Market. We never had enough sweet corn to satisfy buyers. And so one wintry day when we had stopped in town at the café and indulged ourselves with a cup of coffee, we began making rash garden plans.

It seemed so easy, sitting there with the snow swirling outside the window and the caffeine pulsing through our veins, to turn over enough ground and grow enough sweet corn to meet the wants of south central Missouri. Why we could probably even pile up the pickup with it and take it up to St. Louis to sell it at fancy, big-city prices. When we got home, we sat down with the seed catalogue and picked out enough varieties of sweet corn to have a crop ripening over several months. The amount of seed recommended was a lot, I said, as I wrote out the check to pay for it, but then it takes money to make money, we reminded ourselves as we sent off the order.

One day, several weeks later, there was a note in our mailbox reporting that there was a big package for us, too big to be delivered, at the Post Office. We drove into town, wondering what it could be. The postmaster needed some help to heft the bag up on the counter. The bag had a tag on it with our seed company's name.

"What's in here?" he asked, puzzled.

"Oh, just corn seed," I answered, in what I hoped was the offhand manner of someone who regularly planted acres and acres of corn. "We're planning to put in a little extra corn this year."

"Guess you'll be making a still for the squeez-

63

ings," the postmaster said, with a chuckle. We are always doing things that seem slightly unsound by local standards and from his reaction, I guessed that this was one of them.

Early in the spring, Paul hitched up the plow to our old tractor, Alice, while I staked out the piece of pasture land that we were going to devote to our sweet corn project. I nursed agribusiness thoughts as I watched Paul and the tractor appear to grow smaller as he plowed down the length of the field. The plowing was going smoothly, so I started to walk back to the house when I heard a wrenching, metal-breaking noise, followed by certain other noises from Paul that always mean disaster. I ran back to the field to find him standing, fuming, beside the tractor. It was tipped oddly to one side. The rim had broken on one of the big back wheels, the wheel had fallen off, and the tractor had slipped down into a fresh furrow. Paul was mumbling about metal fatigue.

I've noticed that men like to say "metal fatigue" a whole lot to explain mechanical malfunctions. The only thing they like to say better is, "But you can't take that out—it's a bearing wall." Neither can be argued with. I suspect men say those things when they are too tired to think of anything more sensible and they want to silence a troublesome woman.

The tractor looked very heavy, squatting there in the furrow, and I had no idea how we would get it out. Paul rummaged around in the barn and brought out several jacks, including one for a house, and a pry bar of heavy steel. We worked away, alternately jacking, prying, and propping until we righted the tractor. We had it up, but we had no replacement rim. We called it a day, looking sadly at the sky. The weather was perfect for plowing and we weren't sure how long it would hold.

We wanted to get the field plowed on time so that we could get our sweet corn seed planted and make our fortune.

The next day we started out looking for a replacement rim. We visited all the tractor dealers along the highway and found that used rims were hard to find. Farmers usually fill those big back tractor tires with salt water for weight and that rusts the rims. The few used rims that we found were full of holes and subject to metal fatigue. By the end of the day we were one hundred miles from home, in Springfield, at the Allis-Chalmers dealer, a long way from our corn patch. The dealer had a new rim; it was very expensive, but we had to buy it.

Of course, we could deduct the cost from our profits.

It rained for the next three days, but Paul got the tractor back together and when the ground dried out, he finished plowing. I carried the biggest stones out of the field while he disked it with the tractor and prepared a good seed bed. When the weather was warm enough for planting we bought a planter to push along on the big wheels with a hopper for seed. It was expensive, but the field was too big to plant by hand the way we did the garden. I tried to plant the first row. The wheels kept bumping into stones, the furrow maker didn't go deep enough, and the device in back for covering up the seed didn't work. Paul tried the second row with similar results, but he thought if we applied some pressure to the planter, it might work. So we tied a rope to the front of it, I pulled it, and he leaned down on the back of it. It was a hot day and I felt myself getting very cross, especially when he tried to lighten the general mood by calling out "Gee" and "Haw" to me. No, the planter was a failure, so we hung it in the barn and got a couple of hoes. We made the furrows with them, dropped the seed in by hand, and walked back over the rows, tamping the soil down on the corn with the toes of our boots. It took a long time to plant the big field that way.

We hoped we would sell a lot of sweet corn to pay for our time and expenses.

Our regular garden took work, too, and I didn't get around to weeding the sweet corn as often as I should have. The weather was very dry that summer and I began to think that the cover of weeds might be protecting the young corn a bit. We could water our half-acre garden, but there was no way to irrigate the big corn patch. We just let the weeds go.

A friend who grows prize vegetables had heard about our sweet corn project. He came over to see us one day and surveyed the corn patch with all the weeds. "You doing some sort of companion cropping with that corn?" he asked me, his eyes crinkling with amusement.

We stopped talking about trucking sweet corn to St. Louis.

The dry, hot weather continued. The sweet corn leaves turned brown. Even the weeds were wilting. The ears began to form, however. I peeled some open and found them filled with corn earworms. My gardening book said a drop of mineral oil on the silk end of the ear would stop them. I could do that in the small garden, but the corn patch was too big to wander up and down the rows with an eyedropper administering an oily shot in each ear.

As the corn ripened, the earworms were joined by little black beetles and raccoons, all of whom thought our sweet corn patch was a prime place.

I didn't even want to think about sweet corn anymore, but other people did.

We had a little extra sweet corn from our regular garden that we took into the Farmer's Market. Several people said that it was a shame we didn't plant more of it what with all that extra space we had out there on the farm.

The postmaster asked me if we had any extra roasting ears to sell. I pretended I didn't hear him.

At the end of the summer, I spent an afternoon picking the ears that the raccoons had missed. I filled up a couple of peach baskets with the sparse ears and tried to interest the chickens in eating them. They made it quite clear that they preferred the chopped corn that we bought at the feed store, but I refused to buy any more until they ate the sweet corn. That was expensive feed and those old chickens ought to appreciate it.

It was that summer that we bought a coffee pot, too. We are addicted to coffee again and no longer get those wonderful caffeine highs. We can't afford them.

ZUCCHINI ENOUGH

September 16, 1976

Summer is over now and maybe, at last, we'll get some respite from the zucchini, a big, healthy, manic plant that has been sitting in the garden producing squashes without mercy since last June.

The gardening books say that zucchini is a compact summer squash that bears cylindrical fruits with dark green tender skins. The squash are best picked and eaten when they are between six and eight inches long.

But the gardening books never hint at the Zucchini Problem. The zucchini is prolific. With only the tiniest of root systems the plant blooms without surcease all summer long and every trumpet-shaped blossom relentlessly turns into a squash that grows at lightning speed, zipping quickly through the tender stage to become a granddaddy squash, resembling nothing as much as a green baseball bat, with elephantiasis.

The zucchini is a bad practical joke by seed companies who put twenty-five seeds in a packet. The gardening books do caution that a short row of zucchini should be planted, adding in what is the biggest understatement of all horticulture, that the plants are heavy producers.

The first year that we had a garden, I planted four hills of zucchini and was afflicted with zucchini in such great number and size that my friends all started avoiding me. I took to leaving grocery sacks stuffed with oversize zucchini on the doorsteps of total strangers in the dark of night.

The squash bugs that threaten the cantaloupe, the winter squash, and pumpkins don't find the zucchini tasty. The plants don't mind rain; they don't mind drought. They aren't very choosy about the kind of soil they grow in. In fact, they are so easy to grow that every gardener has them. In a rigorous survey of south central Missouri, I have determined that every man, woman, and child has either too many zucchini of his own (and wouldn't you like a few extra?) or has a neighbor who suffers from them.

Tiny, tender young zucchini, sautéed or steamed, are very good if eaten not too regularly. The recipe books list a variety of cunning ways to deal with zucchini past its prime. For the record we have eaten zucchini stew, stuffed zucchini, zucchini casserole, zucchini torte, curried zucchini, and zucchini bread. And I'm getting a little tired of it, thank you.

I have a friend who is a gardener. He tried to slip us some zucchini cookies the other evening when he came over for dinner, but I saw what he was up to and made him eat zucchini pickles until he gave up and promised to take his cookies home.

He is a wood-carver, too, and told us of a novel use for giant zucchini. He carves them, blocking out his rough models before he puts his designs in wood. Generously, I put several of our really big zucchinis in the back of his car when he wasn't looking in case he was running short.

One night this summer when sleep wouldn't come, I was lying in bed wondering about the zucchini's ability to grow so quickly and excessively from tiny green nubbins into two-foot-long squash. I got up to try to catch them at it and tiptoed out to the garden in the moonlight, my feet wet with dew.

But zucchinis have very good hearing, apparently, because when I came up to them, they stopped, held themselves back, and pretended to be just medium-sized summer squash. By the next afternoon, they were huge swollen things, fit to feed only to the chickens, who were beginning to tire of them, too.

The reason I couldn't sleep that night was that I had just finished reading an article about some scientists at Brookhaven Laboratories on Long Island, who have, for the first time, fused human and plant cells and are growing them in a culture there.

Things like that always worry me. I considered various possible crosses. A potato with human cells, for instance, would be unsettling, but probably an introvert. A part-human sunflower couldn't be ignored, but would obviously be a sociable, stately companion. But what would happen if the Brookhaven people start crossing zucchinis and humans? The combination of such plant and animal perversity kept me awake until dawn.

Our only hope is an early frost.

RENT-A-HEAP

—

November 1, 1976

There's a new business out on the West Coast that I read about in the newspaper the other day. It's called Rent-A-Heap. Movie stars and other folks with money, it seems, are bored with driving their well-maintained Mercedes and late-model Rolls Royces, so when they want to draw attention at a film opening or some other big event, they rent a dented rusted old junker from Rent-A-Heap and drive up trailing mufflers and glory and have *such* an amusing story to tell about breaking down on the Santa Monica Freeway.

I was interested to read that story, and I'm sorry that I didn't realize how much fun I'd been having all those years that we have been driving heaps out of economic necessity.

Silly me. I used to commute to work on an interstate highway in a battered old sports car and didn't enjoy it one little bit when the accelerator pedal fell off when I was driving in the left-hand lane. I just didn't see what a lark it was to ease the gradually slowing car across three lanes of fast traffic to get over to the shoulder. I thought all those people honking and shaking their fists at me were angry, but they were just enjoying the fun, I suppose.

It was a mistake, I know now, but I was scared, although not really surprised, because our old heaps have always played pranks on us like that. I've often worried about the steering wheel falling off when I was driving. I asked Paul once what I should do when it did.

"Don't be silly," he said. "That only happens in W. C. Fields movies. Steering wheels can't fall off."

He understands engines, believes in cause and effect, has a firm faith in the perfectability of machinery, and does not subscribe to my principle of mechanics: Solid Metal Breaks; Fastened Metal Comes Undone. He is always surprised and a little hurt when things break down. He is really a very good mechanic and can fix almost anything, but since we have moved to the farm and have a lot of second-hand machinery that gets hard use, things break down faster than he can fix them.

We had a quiet week a while back when everything with wheels peevishly self-destructed. Paul was working hard to get something to run, and I thought of sending an invitation to a movie star to come out and join in the fun and on the way to stop and pick up a pound of butter because we were all out.

There came a day when I scooped out the last of the chicken feed and I was considering revving up the chain saw and driving it to town to buy groceries and feed, but Paul announced that the pickup would run well enough now to take us to town if we were careful with it.

We were halfway to town when some important nut shook loose, and the steering column fell down in his lap.

"You see," I said calmly. It was mean, but I'm only human.

He pushed it back into place with one hand and edged the pickup over to the side of the road. When he was working on it we had a good laugh, of course. What fun it was, we told each other gaily, that our old van threw a rod so that we can't even turn on its engine. How amusing it is that the tractor tire went flat just when the air compressor that could inflate it broke its belt and only screams when plugged in. How diverting that the front springs on the flatbed truck should snap in two just when all these other entertaining things were happening. And now to have the steering wheel fall off the pickup . . . oh, it was just *too* droll.

Times like these make me appreciate that money does not buy happiness. Why, all those movie stars have all that money and they still have to go out and *rent* their heaps. We have them strewn all around our farm. They are our very own.

Paul says that the reason we have these merry times is that we do a lot of driving on rough roads in our beekeeping business. We have to drive over deep ruts, holes, and rocks that shake loose bolts and vibrate vital mechanical parts so that they wear out. He says that even if we bought a new truck, it would shake apart in no time on our Ozark back roads.

Maybe so, but it doesn't seem fair that we should have all this fun. I'm in the market now for a tough, sturdy vehicle, a new one that Paul doesn't have to work on all the time. If any of you hear of a good deal on a Sherman tank under warranty, would you let me know?

Where the Lights
Are Shining

November 12, 1976

We were in St. Louis not long ago and did a lot of big-city stuff. We hissed the Air Force recruiting short at the movies; tried to get dinner at our favorite restaurant, but it was closed; and I got nervous in the five o'clock traffic and jammed on imaginary brakes on the passenger side of the pickup so often that Paul said I'd been in the hills too long.

All in all, St. Louis is a pleasant city, as cities go, and the better we know it, the more we look forward to our trips there. Before we moved to Missouri, I thought of St. Louis as a tuneful, sprigged-muslin sort of place, an impression gained by seeing *Meet Me in St. Louis* as a youngster.

We were relieved to discover that St. Louis isn't quite that wholesome, but on the other hand, it certainly doesn't seem to be as wicked as our Ozark friends and neighbors believe it is. They don't go to St. Louis often. They prefer to have their children go to Kansas City for jobs when they graduate from high school.

When a vacant house is vandalized, the neighbors nod their heads wisely and say that they wouldn't be surprised to hear that loot turned up in St. Louis.

Junk and old tires in our rivers? Someone from St. Louis brought them down special.

Land speculators from St. Louis are usually blamed for driving up the price of land so high that local people can't afford to buy it.

Could it be that local teenagers know more about those funny cigarettes than they should? Rumor has it that there's a shifty-eyed pusher from St. Louis been seen around lately.

When a young man was arrested and tried in the county seat for possession of a controlled substance, he hired a clever lawyer from St. Louis, who, an area newspaper reported sourly, "wore plaid pants" and got the case dismissed.

That same newspaper ran a vivid story about a man from a nearby town who checked into a local motel, was dragged from his bed during the night and roughed up by two men who had kicked in the door. He contended that he didn't know the men and that they escaped without being seen, but the newspaper stated flatly that the unknown assailants "were probably from St. Louis."

There is a story retold here every autumn about a slicker who drove down from St. Louis in his new four-wheel rig and stalked around a farmer's woodlot in his new hunting vest and cap, shooting at deer with his new rifle. Toward the end of the day, he made a hit. He was pretty honest for a St. Louis feller, so he tagged it and took it to the check station where he got riled when the checker told him he'd shot and tagged a goat.

Of course, life isn't just a plate of sunshine cookies here. There aren't any still raids anymore and the fighting, hard-drinking loggers have long since departed. Yet just the other day the local newspaper reported that the police had issued a ticket to a young man "for unnecessary noise and squealing tires." I guess the St. Louis police are kept busy by worse than that, though.

Actually my Ozark friends and neighbors may have a point or two about St. Louis folk.

I've been very cross lately, for instance, about the man who has been buying up farmland near us. He's paid a high price for some rather scrubby land and, although there is much talk, no one knows what he is really going to do with it. He's from St. Louis and I've never met him, but I'd recognize him by the bulge of his money belt and I don't believe I like him.

Then there was that time last deer season when we went to a local café and had to wait a long time because the waitress was serving a dozen men in new hunting vests at the big table. We studied them. They were unfamiliar, perhaps a trifle menacing, probably from St. Louis. The next day I was very careful to keep our pair of Irish setters in the house when I heard shots in the woods. After all, I wouldn't want them to be shot for deer by slickers, or dognapped and taken to St. Louis.

Come to think of it, the next time we go up to St. Louis, I'm going to keep the windows of the pickup rolled up real tight.

STILL NOT
REPUBLICANS

December 2, 1976

This kind of gonzo journalism that I produce about farm life in the Ozarks is not soothing, apparently. A reader wrote, "Doesn't anything ever go right with you people? I worry about you. It all sounds so hard."

Not to worry.

Life isn't hard down here. Things just happen all the time, as I tried to tell my mother not long ago. She had hoped that now that we were middle-aged, she needn't worry about us. For a while we had steady jobs, a regular house, and she hoped that we might even settle down and vote Republican.

Then we chucked it all and became beekeepers in the Ozarks, armed with nothing but our ignorance. She worries. Secretly, of course, she is enjoying it all. It's just the kind of thing she would do. When she turned sixty-five and was forced to retire, she said, "I'll show 'em who's fit," and joined the Peace Corps. She spent a summer taking cold showers and doing calisthenics, and then went off to India for two years.

She'd never ridden a bicycle, but was issued a

crazy pint-sized Russian one with tiny wheels, a So-
viet banana bike. She learned to ride it and pedaled
twelve miles a day on it making her rounds of the
countryside, teaching health and sanitation to rural
Indians.

That was more than ten years ago and today she
holds down two jobs and lives a life so busy that she
makes me tired to think about it. Whenever she can
make time, she comes down here to the Ozarks and
takes care of us. She worries that Paul doesn't get
enough to eat and cooks large and elaborate meals for
him. She says tut-tut to me and warns that I am going
to re-arrange my female organs in some adverse way
by lifting heavy things. She bustles through the house
removing cobwebs and fingerprints that have been
here since her previous visit. The last time she was
here playing lady of the house we were gone most of
the time tending bees.

She was harried taking care of honey customers
and falling behind in her housework when a helicop-
ter landed behind the chicken coop. The dogs were
outraged and barked. The chickens thought it was the
granddaddy of all hawks and went into hysterics.
Mother decided that it was her very first flying saucer
and went out armed with a broom to deal with it. An
ordinary earth man in a business suit got out and asked
if she was interested in selling any walnut timber.

"I thought it was quiet and peaceful out here in
the country," she complained to me afterward.

"Things just keep happening; it's never under
control," I told her.

Well, to all of you who worry, I'd like to announce that for the first time in four years, we're
caught up. Not done, mind you, but caught up. We
haven't had a crisis in two weeks. Our bees are tucked
in for the winter. We've just sold three barrels of
honey to a food co-op. We have two vehicles running
perfectly, something of a miracle as readers will appreciate. We've got enough firewood cut to last through
the winter. There's a cover crop planted in the garden. We've even had time to take a long hike. It's
strange to wake up in the morning and not feel frantic.
I don't know if we can cope with tranquility.

The only problem that we've had is what to name
the new kitten. One night a week ago, just as it was
getting dark, we heard a round of rifle shots on our
road. Paul drove up to see what was happening. As he
approached, some boys with guns drove off quickly in
a pickup leaving behind a terrified black and white
kitten When Paul got out, the kitten rubbed against
him and mewed loudly and insistently. He brought
the kitten home and plunked him down in my lap.
We'll keep him of course. There may have been
others being used for target practice, too, but I don't
want to think about it.

Our other two cats think that he is a terrible idea
and hiss and bat at him, but he doesn't seem to mind.
He's an intrepid creature and picks his way through
our household with cheerful dignity. The dogs are
embarrassed when they wake up to find him purring
contentedly curled up in the concave place between
their hip bones and rib cage. They've tried a growl or

two, but he sweetly ignores them and rubs against their paws.

Naming animals is a serious business with us. The two Irish setters, Farley and Durrell, were named after writers of animal stories. Andy, the beagle (more or less), was named after E. B. White. Our old termagant of a cat, Margaret, was supposed to be given to a young lady named Margaret eleven years ago. So we called her Margaret's cat. The young lady's mother objected. We kept the cat and shortened the name. Tertia, our beautiful but neurotic tortoiseshell cat, was simply the third animal at a time when Brian was reading English boarding school stories.

The new black and white kitten has been nameless now for a week and we have frittered away hours considering names for him. He looks like a perfect Abner, but we had one before and we don't like to repeat.

Don't fret, gentle readers, life is pleasant here in the hills. Instead, why don't you help us think up a name for little Nemo here who is curled up purring on a pile of my typing paper, showing every sign of developing as strong a sense of civil rights as our other animals have.

COLD WRENCHES, WARM HEARTS

December 31, 1976

Everyone knows about those long winter evenings in the country. That's when the family draws close around the wood stove and makes popcorn and munches on crisp apples. That's when cats curl up on laps and purr. That's when there's time to read improving books and think deep thoughts.

Maybe so. But on the long winter evenings, we go out to the barn and rebush the front end of the tractor.

It isn't that I'm a good mechanic, which in these days would be a fine and liberal thing for a woman to be, but I'm the help available. Paul is a good mechanic and a brisk-weather worker. (He also knows a lot of other stuff, is handsome, has a sense of humor, and is soothing to live with. But that's beside the point. Or maybe it isn't.)

No, I'm not a good mechanic. It doesn't have anything to do with the fact that I'm female, understand. I'm sure that there are baby women born every day with a set of socket wrenches clutched in their tiny fists. I simply wasn't one of them. I'm the fumble fingers who couldn't tie her shoes in the first grade. I'm the ninny whose brain turns to test patterns when Paul or Brian explains yet again the intricacies of the internal combustion engine.

My father was the first person who tried to explain to me the workings of gasoline engines when I was just a youngster. He was serious when he spoke of pistons, cylinders, and crankshafts. I was happy that this wonderful person whom I loved so much was talking to me about important and adult matters. I watched his mustache go up and down at the corners of his mouth and said yes, yes, hoping he would continue.

Later, whenever I wanted to be close to him, I would crawl up in his lap, bury my face against his coat, and beg, "Tell me again about the motor in the car." I'd snuggle close and breathe in the joy of having him talk to me, but I never understood a word of what he was saying. After three or four sessions, a pained look would come over his face and I suspect he realized that his daughter was not mechanically inclined.

So, instead, he began to talk botany to me, taking me for long walks in the woods where he would gravely tell the Latin names of all the plants we came across and detail the life cycle of the soldier's cap moss. I forgot the Latin names, they were too hard for an eight-year-old, but he gave me a sense that growing things are special and lovely, not a bad legacy for a girl to have from her father, and perhaps as good a reason as any why I'm sitting out here high on an Ozark hill farm rather than working in an office.

To grow things we need machinery and that machinery must be kept in repair, so I help Paul. Over the years, handing him the nine-sixteenths-inch wrench, holding things in place, and squishing down the valve springs when we rebuild an engine, I've learned a regretful amount of mechanics, enough to be invited out to the barn on a cold winter evening to help with the tractor, enough to worry about odd noises when I drive the pickup.

Some time ago, we loaded up our twenty-five-year-old pickup, Press On Regardless, with dogs and honey and went on a peddling trip to Michigan. We sold all the honey, kept the dogs, and headed back in high spirits through St. Louis, down Interstate 44 to the Ozarks. At St James we decided to stop for gasoline and as we drove off the exit ramp an alarming "clunk, clunk clunk" came from the innards of the truck.

"Rear end?" I suggested to Paul, my good mood fading.

"Rear end," he said sadly.

We found a friendly mechanic who let Paul check out the truck in his garage. The rear end was broken beyond repair. We had three dogs with us, one of them with weak kidneys, and I had a deadline to meet, so we left our pickup at the garage, kissed good-bye to our honey-selling profits, and hired a taxi to take us the ninety miles home. I began to worry.

I knew that a broken rear end was a fatal automotive disease.

I worried after we got home while I tried to write and meet my deadline. "I want 1100 words about a woman in the Ozarks," the editor had said, and added, "Make it funny." How could I explain to her that to a woman in the Ozarks who lacked a rear end, life was not funny, no matter how many sniggers that situation might generate in the editor's New York office. I went on worrying, staring disconsolately at the typewriter.

Paul, however, found a perfectly fine rear end in a junked pickup that was sinking into a farmer's back pasture. He bought it for five dollars, extracted it, and we drove back up to St. James, where he put it in our pickup. I stopped worrying and started writing. Maybe life was funny after all.

Paul says that I'm in a bad place in my mechanical education. He says I know just enough to worry, but not enough to fix things so that I don't have to worry. He pointed that out to me the other evening when he mentioned that work needed to be done on the tractor. He's tried to make it nice for me out in the barn, too. He bought me my very own mechanic's creeper, the deluxe model with a padded headrest, so I can scoot right under a piece of machinery and see what's what. He bought me a pair of insulated coveralls to wear. And this fall he built a cement block chimney on the barn and installed a wood stove to keep it warm out there.

"Besides, what would you rather do?" he asked

when I started explaining about the long winter evenings, about the popcorn, the cats, and the apples.

"What about if I just sit around and be a sex object this evening?" I suggested hopefully.

But no, that wasn't good enough. The steering was bad on the tractor and he needed my help to fix it. With the new wood stove out there it would be cozy, I'd see. I trailed him out to the barn and we lit a fire in the wood stove. One of the cats wandered into the barn and gave me a wry look.

Paul was right, the fire warmed up the cold barn quickly. Not half bad, I thought, as I pulled on my coveralls.

Now if I could just remember where I put that popcorn . . .

SNOWBOUND

February 10, 1977

It won't come as any news, I suppose, to people in St. Louis that we've been having a bit of weather down here in the Ozarks.

Paul and I have been snowed in for twelve days now. Our road is blocked with waist-high snowdrifts at the cliffs that overlook the river. The temperature has been unbelievably low. (Would you believe twenty-seven degrees below zero? No, I thought not. Neither did I until neighbors across the hollow and a friend the next creek over reported the same reading on their thermometers.)

We've tacked rugs over the windows, warmed the water pipes with kerosene lamps, and curled up near the wood stove with big heavy books. There's nothing like wrapping up in a thick Thomas Mann tetralogy to keep out drafts.

We're not suffering any hardships, really, although my typewriter ribbon has gone uncommonly ratty. We have a good supply of life's necessities—

extra feed for the chickens and dogs, firewood, and coffee. Sorry about not boycotting coffee. I did sugar, grapes, beef, lettuce, fur coats, and whales. Someone else is going to have to do coffee.

I have developed an emotional and . . . well . . . close relationship with the wood stove. It sits there grinning its cast-iron door smile and burning warmly, doing its thing in a more lively fashion than anyone else in the family circle at the moment. It is keeping us, quite literally, from freezing to death. That phrase has become cliché for being chilly, but out here behind our drifts, with the wind howling and the temperature sinking, the possibility is a real one outside the circle of heat that the wood stove creates. I respect it and the wood it burns enormously. We have plenty of firewood cut, but it is out in the woodlot, so every couple of days we drive out there and fill the pickup with a load, kicking around in the snowdrifts to find split wood, or sawing up a standing dead tree for seasoned firewood.

All in all we're pretty snug.

Is there an outside world anymore? I begin to wonder. We don't have a television set; our radio burned out a vital transistor last week, and we haven't had any mail delivered for two weeks. I wonder what's happening in Doonesbury? The mailman phones us occasionally to tell us about the fine mail that is piling up down at the Post Office. Today he said he'd try to deliver it, so late in the afternoon I bundled up and whispered the magic question to the dogs, "Want to go for a walk?" They have developed cabin fever and have grown so jittery in our snow-muffled quiet isolation that they throw themselves into a frenzy of defend-the-household barking if an airplane dares fly over or someone has the temerity to start up a chain saw two hollows away. In answer to my question they leapt up, tails wagging, whining with pleasure. My plan was that they would bound on down the road ahead of me and break a path to our mailbox. Not so. They hung behind, waiting for me to break the path and stepped gingerly in my foot-steps. I scowled at them and urged them on ahead but they looked at me soulfully, trying to explain that they were good dogs who knew how to heel very, very well.

I wallowed through the snowdrifts and trudged the two miles to our mailbox only to find it empty and the road by it pristine in its tracklessness. An invigorating and beautiful walk, to be sure, but at the end of it I would have appreciated even junk mail, a flyer offering me a course in locksmithing, or a life insurance plan that I simply could not refuse.

I slogged back home those two miles followed by my sissy dog pack, thinking of the good old days, the days when our mail had a high fun quotient, those days after I had written a column announcing that our biggest problem was naming a new orphan cat. *St. Louis Post-Dispatch* readers took the problem as a chal-lenge and for the next two weeks filled our mailbox with cat names, limericks, funny stories, and observa-tions on other large issues.

The kitten, incidentally, in typically independent,

feline fashion, named himself. When Paul first rescued him he was a slip of a creature, thin and gaunt, but he showed proper appreciation of the food bowl and within a week he began to fill out. He went on eating. Soon he was wider than he was long, wider than he was tall; wideness, indeed, became his most characteristic dimension. And still he ate. He turned into a genuine fatcat. "And what," Paul observed, "could anyone call a fatcat but Grover." So Grover he is and joins the ring of animals close around the wood stove.

It was good to hear from readers, however. Today I'd settle for the *New York Times Year-End Review of Economic Conditions in South America* just to have something in the mailbox.

When the dogs and I got back home, Paul said the mailman had phoned to say that he was sorry that he hadn't been able to make it up the hill to our mailbox. Paul made us hot chocolate and we settled down around the wood stove, first pushing aside the damp laundry draped lankily on chairs, to make great liberating plans about what we are going to do when the snow melts in March.

How am I going to send out this column? I don't know the answer to that, but tomorrow I'm going to ring up the Post Office and see if someone down there won't read me the comics. If Fiorello La Guardia would do it, why not our mailman?

Twenty-three Ways to Close a Fence Gap

February 18, 1977

It was one of those clear, bright, sunny winter days that we have so often in the Ozarks, the kind of day that makes you think up outside work to do, work that didn't seem strictly necessary the day before when it was cloudy.

Paul and I packed a lunch in the morning and headed out to our beeyards. The bees aren't doing much this time of year except clustering in a huddle around the queen and metabolizing fiercely to keep the cluster at ninety degrees, their favorite temperature.

But cows like to scratch their sides against the hives and sometimes knock the hives askew. And skunks pull out the entrance reducers that we wedge in the hive openings in the fall to keep out the mice that chew ragged holes in honeycomb. If skunks can pry out the reducers, they poke a paw into the entrance, stir up the sluggish bees, and pull them out to eat one at a time. So we checked to see that all the hives were in order.

We rent from farmers patches of land for our beehives where good bee forage grows at a cost to us of a gallon of honey a year. We choose hive sites that are protected and away from the road, bee rustling having become an agricultural crime in recent years. In addition to our home yard, we have a dozen or so outyards tucked away in back pastures and woodlots, across rivers, over fords, and behind fences—fences closed in those dozen-odd outyards by twenty-three gates.

I never gave much thought to gates until we started keeping bees in outyards. A gate seems a simple thing, does it not? There are a couple of posts on either side of a gap in the fence and a gate swings between them with a hook to fasten it.

Not so. Not one of those twenty-three gates looks like that. That idealized conception of Gate does not reckon with Ozark ingenuity. Every gate on our rounds is unique. Every fence gap is a new problem to an Ozark farmer, and each problem receives a fresh and novel solution. Even on the same farm one gate has no relationship to its brother gate up the hill.

The prize farm, gatewise, that we visit has three gates that we must drive through. The first one is in two sections, each sturdily and weightily constructed of many, many oak two-by-fours. The gate is closed by weight of the two sections leaning against each other. Thus when the first section is dragged open, the second collapses and pulls out its fence post and a section of fence with it. Oak is very heavy. Closing that gate is an exercise in fence building every time we go there.

The second gate is built in layers. The first layer is a light, mimsy, three-strand section of barbed wire stretched in a highly hypothetical way over three poles and fastened at the post side with a twist of coat hanger. Resting partly across the wire is an oak fence section. To open the gate, we must drag away the fence section and then unhook the coat hanger, being careful to catch the wire quickly so that it won't snarl before it is closed again.

The final gate is a gate more in theory than in practice. It is three separate strands of barbed wire flung at the fence gap and held in place by moral suasion. Opening and closing it is a problem in metaphysics, not farming.

We have hives at a prosperous 1,000-acre cattle ranch. The gate that we have to drive through there was at one time well balanced and, although made of oak, swung open easily from its stylish horseshoe hook fastener.

The hands at the ranch are tall, strapping men who ride herd wearing chaps over their jeans and probably pose for Marlboro ads after hours. They are very strong and apparently don't mind that the vital fence post holding this gate has relaxed a bit so that the heavy oak gate now must be dragged across the ground when it is opened or closed. It is a gate to tone the muscles, to build the body. Maybe that's how the cowboys got so muscular there.

One of our yards has a lightweight, well-balanced metal gate, straight from the farm supply store, but it is padlocked and we can't get in there at all if I've left the key in the pocket of my other jeans.

Beyond the gate is an opening in the fence with an impossibly heavy cattle oiler dripping insecticide stretched between the two posts. I can, and have, pulled it up the two inches past taut to get it off its hook and heaved it over to the other post, but Paul usually lifts it off to keep me from being insufferable, to stop me from flexing my biceps at total strangers and boasting that that was one heavy cattle oiler I just hefted.

One yard has a gate closed with a hinged horse collar. To open it is an I.Q. test that I have flunked.

There are others: the electric gate, the Arkansas gate fastened with a bit of wire and a stick to provide the leverage to close it; the concrete reinforcing wire mesh gate tied closed with baling twine. But you get the picture. Twenty-three fence gaps and twenty-three ways to close them, all testimony to Ozark inventiveness and anarchy.

The first rule of country living is to leave gates as you've found them, opened, closed, or somewhere in between. We do, 'course, but it isn't easy.

WHY I NEEDED
A STONE FLOOR

April 21, 1977

Our termites swarmed up from the living room floor and out of the walls yesterday. They do it every spring. It's reassuring proof that the earth continues to spin and tilt and that summer is on its way.

From a natural-history point of view, termites are interesting creatures. For instance, before I became so closely acquainted with them, I never would have guessed that there are twenty-one hundred species of termites in the world but only forty-one in North America. Or that termites are able to eat wood fibers only because the protozoa that live in their stomachs digest it for them. That although termites are often called white ants, they are not ants, and often they are not white. Or even that termite colonies are divided into castes: soldiers, workers, and reproducers. It is the reproductive termites that swarm out of our wood-work on wing. If they can find a suitable place to set up housekeeping, they shed their wings, form pairs, and begin a new colony.

All that is very instructive to be sure, but does not hide the fact that year after year, our house is becoming more insubstantial. The original cabin that is now our living room was built on the bare ground, so the termites under it don't have to send out for dinner. They just chew on the floor whenever they are hungry. The other three rooms of our house were built later on concrete slabs. Unfortunately, whoever poured the concrete neglected to take out the wooden forms around the edges. The termites found those forms very tasty and after they had polished them off, they proceeded on up into the house sills and studs.

Paul figures that the first three feet of the house all the way round is pretty well riddled by termites, but that the rest of it is still sound. Someday, quite soon now, we are going to have to jack up the whole house, cut out the bottom yard of wall, rip up the living room floor, and fix up the whole place.

It's a funny little house in many ways. In addition to the generally spongy condition of the wood throughout, there are the windows that don't really open and don't really close. The kitchen counter fits rather less than more against the wall which is not quite straight. The plumbing is odd and creative.

One end of the house is made of tiny stones, seashells, flower pots, dime-store jewelry, and bottle caps, all held in place with generous daubs of mortar. There is a screen in one of the windows at that end, and it, too, is mortared in place. That is very secure, of course, but the thick lip of mortar around the screen traps water inside during a rainstorm—water that then runs down inside the house. Cleverly, I've put a row of house plants under that window so that they are watered every time it rains. Paul's typewriter also sits under the window and also is watered.

We bought our farm and this house from Louise and Earl. Louise had lived here all her life; she was born in a log house to the south of the present house. Her parents homesteaded the place. Louise and Earl built the cabin with materials scavenged from the log house and added to it, lovingly, building with whatever materials were at hand and plenty of very large nails.

Earl was a big man and he liked big nails; sixty-penny nails, six-inch-long spikes, were his favorites above all others. He used them to sustain the main beams as well as to tack up pieces of thin linoleum or to hang a picture. When we moved in, we found a big stack of oak four-by-fours out in the barn, bristling with sixty-penny nails driven halfway, apparently just for fun and practice. Louise said Earl spent a lot of time out in the barn talking to the mule. Earl was good with mules and children, she reported.

Louise and Earl lived here in amity with a mule and a pair of pigs named Jack and Jackie. They planted daffodils throughout the woods. They tried to keep cows, but that didn't work out, so they put out a salt lick for the deer instead. They tramped the hollows and washed their laundry in the river. They made jelly from the wild blackberries and canned wild greens. They never were successful with chickens, but they fed chopped corn to the flock of wild turkeys. They tamed a box turtle so that it would come up to the doorstep and beg for toast crumbs. Louise told us about the whippoorwill that would wait at the kitchen door each evening for Earl to accompany him to and from the outhouse.

At first I wrote off that last tale to a lively Ozark imagination. Whippoorwills, according to my bird book, are shy and are seldom seen by human beings. But every evening that first spring and summer that we lived here, a whippoorwill would appear at the kitchen door and stand there agitatedly calling whip-poor-will-whip-poor-will-whip-poor-will-whip-whip-whip, ignoring us when we turned on the light to look at him and wandering off disconsolately after an hour or so.

Louise and Earl were poor, and so by some standards they weren't very successful farmers, but they were happy here. They wore out the soil, but they put down a layer of peace, harmony, and good karma so thick that you can feel it swirl up around as you walk through a shimmering field of daisies in the old pasture on a summer moonlit night.

Someday we'll build with stone and concrete and not have termites, I guess, but not today. Today I'm going out in the woods and watch the daffodils bloom.

MO MO

Last winter the Academy of Applied Science, a group
of engineers and scientists in Boston, folded up its
expedition and stole away from Loch Ness, conclud-
ing after almost a year of peering and listening with
camera, sonar, computer, hydrophone, and diving
gear, that there might be a monster in the Loch, but
then again, there might not.

Like most people, I guess, I prefer to deal with the
monsters without rather than those within, so it is
always cheering to learn that they still may be out
there and are baffling the experts.

The Academy of Applied Science researchers are
going back to Scotland for another go at the Loch
Ness monster this spring because, as the leaders of the
expedition solemnly say, there's still "something large
and mysterious" happening in the depths of the Loch.

A Nessie recently turned up in a lake in Kazakh,
USSR, near Alma-Ata, and the impeccable observer,
a Russian biologist, in usual monster-witness fashion,

forgot to take a picture of it with the camera that was hanging on a strap around his neck.

I also read that the trackers in this country are gearing up in the Northwest to make another attempt to hunt down the Sasquatch, or Big Foot, or Yeti, that huge, hairy manlike creature that inhabits the fringes of the mind as well as, possibly, the Pacific Northwest, the Himalayas, and the Ozarks.

There is a long tradition of Sasquatch sightings in this part of the country and because everyone else is investigating monsters, I think I should contribute my own report, a modest bit of research that proves that in the monster line, as well as most other things, Missouri is way out front.

For the sake of scientific accuracy, I should point out that my sightings did not occur on a wild scramble up cliff and crag, but in the comfort of the brown leather chair while I was thumbing through a collection of old local newspapers a few evenings ago.

The paper in its June 26, 1925, edition reports:

WILD MAN EXCITEMENT

. . . More or less excitement has been caused the past three or four weeks by reports coming here that a wild man, ape or gorilla had been seen east and north of Alton by the farmers out in that neighborhood.

The first report coming in was that a peculiar-looking beast crossed the state highway some three weeks ago and was noticed by some of the road hands. A little later, parties out northeast of town had seen something in the woods that walked upright like a man, that soon disappeared in the thick undergrowth and was lost sight of. However, the latest report comes from Lewis Botes, who lives two miles out on Greer road, who says last Wednesday his children first saw it and told him about it. He went out to where they told him it was and got within about 50 yards of it and was able to see it plainly, and he terms it an animal that walks upright like a man, rather brown hair all over and had a face something like a monkey.

He said that when he tried to ride closer to it, it ran and was soon lost sight of in the thick brush.

The "beast" then took his big feet, evidently, and headed north about 220 miles, for on August 13, 1925, the *Standard* published this item:

WILD MAN MYSTERY SOLVED

The mystery of a "wild man" scare near Alton, in Oregon county a few weeks ago, is believed to have been solved by the confession of a "wild man" taken in charge by officers at Chillicothe.

Following reports that something resembling a "wild man" had been seen lurking in the brush near Chillicothe, officers from that place went in search of the man and found him sitting under a tree fanning himself. He was taken to Chillicothe, but later turned loose and told to clear out . . .

The man's face was covered with a two-month's growth of black beard, his clothing torn and old. The open shirt revealed that his breast was covered with a growth of hair fully six inches long and badly matted. Further examination showed his body to be entirely covered with hair.

His face resembles that of a monkey and Sheriff Dowell said had he appeared hatless and naked in that vicinity, he could in reality have been mistaken for a creature half monkey and half man.

The man, who was 57 years of age, was very reluctant [sic] and seemed to be suffering from mental aberration, but admitted that he had been in the vicinity of Alton, Mo., in the southern part of the state several weeks ago when workmen on the highway claimed to have seen a wild man skulking in that vicinity a number of times. One man claimed he came within fifty feet of the man, who ran away, walking like a huge orangoutang.

Lewis Botes has disappeared from Alton. I rang up the sheriff's office in Chillicothe, but no one there remembers about the Wild Man. Sheriff Mott Dowell, the folks in the office say, is retired and "probably somewhere in Arizona," so I didn't get to share his reminiscences. I'm sorry, because he strikes me as the typical Missouri lawman, a cautious and unflappable man. He apprehended an unusual creature. It wasn't doing any harm. He examined it, satisfied his own curiosity, and told it to "clear out."

Note, please, that he did not announce that a Jungian Archetype had wandered into town. He didn't phone a university anthropologist, or even a public relations man. He did not, apparently, write a report for a learned journal. He'd mind his business if the Sasquatch would mind his. Better to keep the monsters moving on, "turned loose" and out there. Sheriff Dowell must be a man with respect for monsters and may have realized that if he didn't turn loose this one, there would be all that trouble of inventing another.

The Academy of Applied Science would do a lot worse than to take along a Missouri sheriff on its spring expedition.

THE CURSE OF MOSES

May 19, 1977

There was a story in the *Post-Dispatch* a while back from Eldon, Missouri, a town just north of Lake of the Ozarks. The Board of Education there banned the American Heritage Dictionary for use in its junior high school because the dictionary contained 39 four-letter words that shocked a group of two dozen Eldon adults when they looked them up and copied them.

There was some editorial tut-tutting in the *Post* about this latter-day Comstockery, but the newspaper didn't report what those thirty-nine words are.

Since the Berkeley Free Speech Movement worked its way across the country, flowing through drawing rooms and slithering in and out of the wire-taps at the White House, I didn't know that there was even a single indelicate word left— let alone thirty-nine.

My curiosity piqued, I sat down with a pencil and on the back of an old envelope made a list of four-letter words that might possibly raise eyebrows in

Eldon. All I could come up with were fifteen. I lack either the sensibilities or the experience of one of the leaders of the protest against the dictionary. He said that people shouldn't look up blue words in the dictionary, even though he had; they should learn them, he said, just like he did, "in the gutter." I haven't spent my time in the right places, I guess, but I do wonder what those other twenty-four words are.

Everything considered, cussing is pretty dreary these days.

Blasphemy won't satisfy anymore. Pick a deity from any pantheon and try to work up a good strong anathema. You might just as well stick to "by Jove" for all the fun you'll get from it.

Obscenities are all overworked, poor, thin and tired. White-haired grandmothers and American presidents use dirty words with about as much force (and probably as little relief to the soul) as my maiden aunt when she handed out "Mercy" to express her inner turmoil.

When there were still some wicked words, there was something rather cheering about letting one rip in a true emergency. Still, they were never anything more than shorthand; they gave only a kind of temporary comfort, nothing compared to what a well-constructed, thoughtful curse could do.

It's rather healthy, I suspect, to take Wrath, run it through the brain cells, condense it, organize it, trim it up, and select a whole railroad train of words to give it form.

I found just such a curse recently, an Ozark mas-

terpiece of emotion as well as literature. It is written
in ink now brown on yellowing rag paper and fell out
of an 1893 atlas that I had the good fortune to buy at
a country auction for a nickel.

I'd like to share it with readers who might feel the
occasional need for strong language.

> heres hoping that all muggon misers lyars ta-
> tlers and back biters may all be rammd gammd
> and damnd into the north corner of hell there
> to set with brimsone sulphur smoke and ashes
> to be blowed in their eyes and after that to be
> chased round hell with a butchers block slung
> to their arzes and all the hounds in america in
> full cry after them and after being chased
> round there a thousand years them that will
> speake anything in their praise may they be
> toss into the sharks belly and the shark into the
> whales belly and the whale into the devils
> belly and the devil into hell and the door
> locked and the key lost and a blind man look-
> ing for it Moses

Now there's a fresh, rich, full-bodied malediction.
The creative spelling, the lack of punctuation and the
sprightly grammar all point to it being an original.

But how is a muggon miser to be gammd? And for
that matter, what nasty, transcending trait does an
ordinary, everyday, run-of-the-market miser have to
be labeled "*muggon*"?

I don't while away my time looking up dirty

words in the dictionary, but that's where I go when I come across a word I don't know. After rummaging through a variety of dictionaries, I found "gam" is an old whaling word. It originally meant a gathering of whales at sea, but came to be extended to a meeting of whalers at sea. When whalers drew their boats together to chat and gossip, it was called gamming.

The Oxford English Dictionary, lapsing into a bittersweet, landlubberly mood, refers to gamming as "a relic of one of the most romantic, and perhaps pathetic, phases of the whaler's life." The whalers gave the word to American speech and gamming came to mean getting together to gossip on land as well as sea.

Moses wanted his enemies, those lyars, tatlers, and back biters to gam themselves right into perdition.

Muggon is apparently a victim of Moses' spelling and is bent from neither "moggan" (a long stocking), nor "muggles" (a woman of easy virtue), but most probably from "muggins," a fool, a simpleton. To "talk muggins" is to say silly, foolish things. Misers who were muggon misers must have spread foolish irresponsible tales, gamming about poor Moses right along with all those other dreadful people.

I picture Moses as a retired seafaring man who had bought a small farm in the Ozarks. I see him, a man beset with money problems and with gossips as neighbors, a man in high dudgeon, working up this curse, his brow furrowed in concentration, searching for the right word, crossing out one phrase, substituting another, smiling when he came up with a tuneful bit of alliteration, and then copying it all out in a fair hand, a man mightily relieved.

I don't think that there are any words in it that the folks in Eldon would object to.

I'd like to offer it to them.

I think I've had my nickel's worth.

SUFFICIENCY
AND SUFFICERS

———

June 9, 1977

A woman with whom I have a nodding acquaintance stopped me on the street the other day.

"You're one o' them back-to-the-land people, I hear, so self-sufficient and all, I'd like to ask you a question," she began.

My stomach started to tighten the way it always does when I'm required to answer objective test questions.

"What kind of vegetable juicer should I buy?" she asked.

"Vegetable juicer?" I repeated, stalling for time.

"Oh, *you* know," she said impatiently. "I want to make me some carrot juice, but I don't know what kind of juicer to buy."

I reached around inside my head, hoping a sensible thought might be found somewhere.

"Once, back in 1946 a woman tried to make me drink a glass of celery juice," I said. "I poured it in her Boston fern. It didn't hurt the fern, but it tasted awful."

It was the sole item my brain had on file on vegetable juice. It didn't serve. The woman looked at me, disappointed.

"I was sure you'd know about vegetable juicers," she murmured as she walked away.

I went home and looked in the mirror. There it was. That face with crows' feet around the eyes. Chin starting to sag. Hair with split ends. Did that look like a face that drank carrot juice? No, I reassured myself, it did not.

That was the day I decided I'd write a serious column about the back-to-the-land mystique, about self-sufficiency. Away with scorn and mocking laughter. I'd write a thoughtful and well-reasoned column saying that self-sufficiency was a myth, promoted by slick magazines. I'd mention that this is a tiny, crowded, interdependent world, that it is impossible to be self-sufficient after you have used one factory-made steel nail, made one telephone call, bought one vegetable juicer, eaten one pizza.

I'd write that it was foolishness to believe that folks who grew their own asparagus had any secrets of health and happiness. I'd work up the theme that the back-to-the-land movement trades on fear, timidity, fallout shelter syndrome, and the delusion that somehow, having made a nasty mess of our times, it is possible to step out of this decade, this century, back into a simpler technology, a less populous, unspoiled America, a golden age of about 1880.

Yes, and then I'd add a graceful and instructive bit about how the time just before the turn of the century was not the Golden Age, but the Gilded Age.

Self-sufficient, vegetable juicer lady? Don't lay that trip on me. At best, I'm amusing myself; at worst, running scared.

It would be a tiresome column, but it would be very serious.

I sat down to write it, but the words wouldn't come. I pushed back the typewriter and started idly leafing through the *Post-Dispatch*, which had just come in the mail.

I came across a story in the paper headlined "Ex-Professor Finds Joy in the Ozarks." That came close to home, so I read it with attention. The story was about a man and his family who had moved to the Ozarks to escape the consumer economy. They worked hard for three years and now grow their own vegetables, keep their own chickens, generate their own electricity with a wood-fired steam generator, plow with oxen, and bake in a solar-heated oven.

It appeared that this clever family had been very successful at extricating themselves from the commercial world of mall and marketplace, so successful, in fact, that they entered a self-sufficiency contest, a kind of back-to-the-land bake-off, sponsored by *Mother Earth News*. *Mother Earth News* is a magazine that has pleaded ably the cause of the simple life and self-sufficiency and has prospered enough in doing it that staffers fly on editorial rounds in their very own *Mother Earth News* Lear jet, an airplane that is not methane powered.

The Ozark family was so wonderfully independent that it beat out 286 other aspiring self-sufficers and won the contest.

They won the first prize. And was the first prize for cutting themselves off from a money economy a bag of brown rice? It was not. Was it a ton of old aluminum printing plates from the *Mother Earth* presses suitable for roofing a house? Or a dump truck full of autumn leaves for the compost pile? It was not.

It was ten thousand dollars.

I hope that family has the wit and style to blow it all on a luxury cruise to the Caribbean.

It was then that I gave up on my column. There are some topics that will simply not yield to solemnity.

ALL THE HOURS

June 15, 1977

I'll never be an Ozarker.

Oh, I've come a long way since that first day Paul and I moved to these hills and a new friend was telling us an outrageous story about someone he called an "old boy" and I assumed he was talking about an alumnus of a good boarding school who wore a regimental striped tie.

Now years and a Southern president later, I know that he was talking about a man wise in the ways of country living, a man who knew his pickups and hounds, a clever and capable man, a man who routinely produced silk purses from sows' ears because sows' ears were the materials at hand.

I've learned to pronounce the word "route" as "rowt," not "root." Thanks to the *Post-Dispatch*, I now type "drouth," not "drought." I'm a fidgety person, but I've learned to "set awhile" in a proffered rocking chair when we go to visit a neighbor before conducting the business that is the purpose of the call.

But I'll never be an Ozarker. I can't keep the hours.

The other day, I overheard one old boy in the hardware store ask another how he liked life now that he had retired from farming and moved into town.

"Just fine," the other replied. "Course there's not much to do. Why sometimes I lie abed until seven of a morning."

The first old boy shook his head in disbelief, hardly able to comprehend what slothful luxury it would be to lie abed until seven.

Many of the stores in town are said to open at seven, a situation that I am unable to report firsthand because I've never been there at that time.

Our Ozark friends and neighbors, gentle and polite people, are tolerant of our outlandish hours, and take great pains to accommodate us. When they come over at 6:30 in the morning to pay a call and perhaps buy a dozen eggs or a pound of honey, they honk the horn on their pickups extra long and extra loud and then wait a few minutes to give us time to roll out of bed before they pound on the door.

I don't really know what time they get up. I've been afraid to ask. But I've heard talk about things that happen at four and five in the morning and there are some dairy farmers that we know who say they begin their day at three-thirty, but I think that they must be fibbing.

Of course, Ozark people taper off pretty early in the afternoon, too. Stores close up tight at five. Everyone goes home, eats supper, and goes to bed. Houses are dark in the evenings and the streets of town are quiet and empty except for a few teenagers who cruise the darkened three-block downtown in a desultory way, occasionally stopping in groups of three and four to lounge on the hoods of their cars, waiting vainly, but patiently, for something to happen.

We made arrangements to set up a bee outyard with a farmer not long ago. We cleared a site in the afternoon and stopped by his house to tell him we'd be moving the beehives sometime that week in the evening when it was dark, after all the field bees had come back to their hives. We offered to telephone before we came so that he would know who was driving through his pasture at night.

"Why, you don't need to phone," he said. "We stay up late—almost to eight-thirty every evening."

We've never let on that we stay up until ten or even worse.

There are, to be sure, certain dark, macho, night-time activities that raise no eyebrows in the Ozarks. These include running hounds; coon and coyote hunting; gigging or night fishing, which is legal here in the winter; spotlighting deer, which is illegal; and a certain amount of heavy, sodden drinking in parked pickups.

But to stay up at night, using the electric lights and constructing beehives, reading, rebuilding a truck engine, extracting honey or even having dinner at eleven P.M., which we often do in the summer, would be considered peculiar, exotic, unsound, and somehow degenerate.

In the daylight, I can fit in quite nicely, now. I sit there rocking in a chair, slinging out "drouth" and "rowt," laughing and telling lies along with the best of them, but it's those dim, electric-lit hours that are the test, a test I'll never pass.

I knew that of a certainty this morning. The telephone rang at six. The caller really just wanted to know whether Paul had that old busted transmission and if a man could buy the casing. But he was polite, considerate, and full of patient, condescending Ozark understanding of effete outlander ways. He knew better than to plunge right in with hard questions like "Nice morning, isn't it?" or "Have you ever seen such a year for alfalfa weevils?" or any such typical conversation openers. No, what he asked, after I'd thought very hard and come up with a wooly hello, was:

"Are . . . you awake?"

It's a question he'd never ask a real Ozarker.

June 29, 1977

Today is as good a day as any to think about Buck Nelson, Mountain View's most famous resident. Of course June 24 would have been better because that is Flying Saucer Day and Buck Nelson claimed he took a ride in one, but sometimes I get behind in my thinking.

June 24 is celebrated as Flying Saucer Day by folks interested in that sort of thing and more punctual in their musings than I am, because that is the anniversary of the day that "Flying Saucer" first floated into American speech.

On June 24, 1947, a businessman, piloting his own airplane over the Rocky Mountains, spotted a cluster of metallic-looking, wingless objects, flying in formation. He described them to newsmen, saying that their motion appeared to be "like a saucer . . . skipped across the water." The news services garbled the quote, bored earthlings snatched it up, and Flying Saucers were born.

Buck Nelson, a bachelor, had traveled and worked in forty-eight states before he decided to settle down on a farm near our town. He was, by all accounts, a conservative, religious man, apparently something of a loner. His story, roughly, follows.

He was fifty-nine in 1954 when he had his first contact with Saucer folk. They didn't land at his place then, but shot "rays" at him, which tumbled him over behind a barrel and cured him of his rheumatism. They promised, in English, to return. He had a couple of other spacey visits, and then, in the spring of the following year, a Flying Saucer landed on his farm and its crew came into his house for a chat. They were a mixed lot and included one old and wrinkled mute who was a space pilot trainee, a 200-year-old spaceman with the disappointingly mundane name of Bob Solomon, a teenage human being who had dropped out and spent the two previous years living on Venus, and a 395-pound dog named Bo.

Having Space Folk in was, evidently, like having a visit from an intergalactic Heloise. Buck said:

They were interested in everything about the house . . . My bed, for instance, has dust under it . . . They told me, and I later saw how their beds were built half in the wall. There were not blankets or sheets to wash, nor even bed making to do . . . Even the pillow was part of the mattress . . . with a soft, smooth washable surface. All this, they explained to me made less work and a more comfortable home.

After a few more household hints and the dictation of twelve laws of God and a twenty-page Bible, the Space People invited Buck for a spin in their Flying Saucer.

They first visited Mars, where their craft dipped low to give Buck, who had spent some of his itinerant years as a rancher, a good chance to look at the Martian cows grazing on Martian grass in the Martian fields. After they landed, he paid a call on one of the Martian rulers, who was wearing bib overalls.

On Venus, Buck was enchanted with the cars that skimmed over the land without wheels, eliminating the need for roads and traffic policemen. Without policemen, he observed, there were no crimes, no jails. And without police, jails, crime, and roads, the taxes were very low, so low that he said Venusian taxes compared to the Earth's "like a nickel to a dollar."

On the Moon, he inspected the hangars on the bases for interplanetary travel.

Despite the fine tax setup on Venus, Buck returned to Earth, where he lost no time in spreading the story of his adventures. He wrote a book and began lecturing, advocating the twelve rules of God and preaching a life free from tobacco, coffee, tea, drugs, and disease.

Some of Buck's friends helped him organize a Space Craft Convention, a three-day affair held at Buck's farm, which became a regular event each year the last week in June. Saucer Faithful came from all over the country to attend. Tourists are tourists, whether they want to float the rivers, shoot deer, or look at a Flying Saucer landing site, so the local people turned out to cook for the conventioners, and run the concession stands at Buck's farm, selling soft drinks and food to the hungry and souvenirs to those whom they could.

Buck himself had a concession booth where he sold "rods with bedspring formations."

The 1961 convention was highlighted by an unusual event. According to the local newspaper

A strange and wonderful phenomenon was demonstrated by the Space People Saturday night at 11 P.M. There was a radio-active fall-out that made many itch all over until a shower of thin silver slivers that looked like bits of aluminum fell from the sky. They glistened in the moonlight as they wiggled down from a spaceship that dropped them to nullify the radio-activity. People were picking them up all the next day to take home as souvenirs—only they disintegrated the next day.

Buck built an enthusiastic cult of followers and continued to hold space conventions, selling his bedsprings and soft drinks until 1964, despite the raised eyebrows of a fair number of Show Me skeptics. Eventually he moved on to the more congenial surroundings of Southern California.

Some of Buck's followers still live here and wait for the Space Men to return. They have given the area a certain cachet and attracted others interested in exploring the murky fringes of reality and delusion. Guarded references to Flying Saucer sightings crop up in conversations now and then, but no moves have been made to hold Space Craft Conventions again.

Buck Nelson is dead now. I drove over to his farm, a few hills and hollows from ours, the other day to look around. Nothing unusual has ever happened there in the memory of the present owners of the land. The concession stands are boarded up and rotting. The soft drink machines are rusting. Weeds grow everywhere.

It's a shame. You'd think those tidy Space People would stop by and spruce up the place.

THE PENULTIMATE GARDEN

August 11, 1977

I spent some time the other afternoon out in the garden tracking the Swiss chard. I know it's out there. It can't escape me much longer. I've got a good idea of weed groupings now, so it's just a matter of time until I find it.

This is a very different garden from our first one. I knew where things were in that garden; each row was labeled. Paul drew a floor plan of it. We had no elusive vegetables.

We bought our farm at the end of April that year and were determined to put in a garden before we drove to Rhode Island to pack up our possessions and move back out here for good.

We set to work with a few hand tools, digging up a sunny, but turfy spot where Louise and Earl, who had owned the place, had once grown a garden. It was hard work to turn over the sod, break up the clods, and rake out a seed bed. Our muscles were enormously surprised.

Louise watched us for a while as we were spading, blistering, forking, aching, raking, and sweating.

She took me aside, shocked. "That's man's work. That's plowing," she explained. "Women make gardens all right, but menfolk do the plowing."

After we had lived here for a while, I discovered that she was pretty much right. To be sure, there are some crackerjack male gardeners in the Ozarks, but for the most part, men prepare the garden and then turn it over to the women who grow all the vegetables except potatoes.

Men usually plant, hoe, and harvest the potatoes. Potatoes are the vital item in the male Ozark diet, a three-times-a-day feature on the menu, only occasionally being displaced at breakfast by heavy, filling servings of biscuits and gravy. I suspect that men believe that potatoes are too important to be left to women who are insufficiently interested in them and might not grow enough potatoes if left on their own.

I disregarded Louise's observation. Strictly speaking, our first garden was a rather small one. Working by hand, it took the two of us softies an entire week to prepare a seed bed. Blistered, sore, and incredibly weary, we staggered around it the last day before we had to leave, planting our seeds and covering the entire garden with a foot of straw mulch.

We were gone for a month and when we returned the garden was beautiful, suggesting that the real secret to gardening success is to plant it and then abandon it.

It was a fine garden for a first attempt, and spurred

us on in the following years to righteous soil improvement, bigger gardens, more grandiose gardens, heavy commitments as vegetable suppliers to folks in town, and nervous exhaustion.

So this was to be the year of Less Garden. When the seed catalogues came in January, I reminded myself to keep my priorities straight. After all, we were making our living keeping bees and they need attention at the same time a garden does. I held myself in tow fairly well. With snow swirling outside and the seed catalogues spread out before me, I successfully fought off the desire to be the first in my neighborhood to grow a baobab tree, crossed out the order for vegetable spaghetti that my hand wrote all by itself, was severe with myself when I began thinking about growing luffa sponges. I ordered a few packets of sensible seeds and, as a reward, a lot of flowers. After all, flowers don't need to be canned.

In March I sowed most of the garden to sweet clover and tilled a little patch for flowers and vegetables.

Our friend, Flummer, who is a good gardener, came down for a visit. "Fallow," I explained guiltily. "I'm letting it go fallow this year. You know, crop rotation, and all that."

He looked amused. Our gardening always amuses him.

"What are a few weeds?" I asked myself in April as the dainty lambs' quarters and tiny pigweeds began to sprout. We had bees to feed, hives to be divided.

"The flowers are pretty and the vegetables can

hold their own," I said in May. We were busy putting supers on the beehives.

But now is the time of truth in the garden.

Two days of showers turned those innocent weeds of April into Missouri's first rain forest, a situation that I should report to the Smithsonian.

Every third darling carrot has peevishly turned itself into a giant Queen Anne's lace, thriving in the rich garden soil. The pumpkins have surreptitiously lunged out of their places in the sweet corn and are throttling the tomatoes.

Flummer came for another weekend visit to see how the crops were rotating. I confessed to him that I had lost the Swiss chard, but I hurried to point out that in my search for it I had come across some green beans that I'd forgotten.

He laughed. He never loses things in his garden, never discovers a vegetable that had slipped his mind. His garden never needs to be reported to the Smithsonian.

That laughter stung. I'll find that chard, I will. I'm going out there in the garden armed with a machete and a pigweed attack dog. My mind's made up. There's no turning back.

But if you don't hear from me by the end of the growing season, would someone please send in native bearers?

I'm Not An Artichoke

August 30, 1977

I'm a lousy cook.

It's an embarrassment because this column appears in a part of the *Post-Dispatch* that's heavily laced with food features from which I avert my eyes as I thumb my way toward Doonesbury. I worry that I'm not doing my part.

Sometimes I wish that I could work up an interest in Lamb Goulash au Blanc or be able to offer a hint on the construction of the perfect flan. Sometimes, but not very often.

My lack of skills and interest stems from the long years I spent as a working motherperson when cooking was geared to immediate satisfaction of severe physical needs and not at all a creative-sense experience.

That perfectly delightful son whom I brought home from school each day on my way back from work, that witty, intelligent charming conversationalist with whom I shared an hour's drive and discussions on the Athenian constitution, French conjugations, and the biology of the frog, would turn on me the minute we stepped in the front door and ask "How long until dinner?" before I'd had time to shift mental gears or even slip out of my high-heeled shoes (yes, heels).

His father would drive in at about the same time with a pinched and hungry look, the pair of them reminding me of hungry baby birds with their beaks open. I would teeter around the kitchen in my heels, fixing something to eat and silently asking my XX chromosomes, Why Me? Why Me? Those were the days before The Movement, you understand.

One of the delights of having a male child is the very long period of time during which it is utterly unimportant what is on the table to eat, just so there is lots of it. In those days Fast and Enough were the only two factors I considered when I planned (!) meals.

The male child grew up and is now a handsome, charming, witty, and intelligent young man who no longer eats at home. He has become a first-rate cook and his father makes waffles that are out of this world. Somehow my culinary skills never blossomed.

I was sure when we retired and moved to the country I'd have time to clip recipes, experiment with ingredients, and stir the soup pot. But the hours slip by and you'd be surprised how tasty crackers and peanut butter are after a long day working in bee outyards. Fast and Enough.

All this is an apologetic introduction to a recipe

128

that I have to offer. Hoyt Alden,* read no further.

A friend of ours was down at the Saturday morning auction a few weeks ago and, seized with madness, bid fifteen cents for a case of canned artichokes. He won the bid.

He unloaded a half dozen tins of the damned things on us. We'd eaten fresh artichokes in France, dipping the leaves in melted butter, but they weren't anything like the ones in the tins. The canned ones were dreadful, tiny, soggy, and lacking taste and pizazz. With my waste-not, want-not outlook I thought it was immoral to throw them away, yet I couldn't figure out what to do with them.

Then, wonderfully, that night Pat Nixon appeared to me in a dream and said she'd like to give me Dick's favorite recipe for tinned artichokes. Honest, this is all true. Besides this is the only benefit I've ever received from Richard Nixon. I'd like to share it with readers.

RICHARD NIXON ARTICHOKES

All the tinned artichokes you want to
    get rid of
Green beans to suit
Butter
A whole lot of sour cream
One handful of slivered almonds
Sauté artichokes in butter. Add cooked
    green beans and almonds.
Stir in sour cream, heat, and serve.

---

*Hoyt Alden was the *St. Louis Post-Dispatch* food writer in those days.

As Pat Nixon faded away in my dream, she called out, "Don't forget the almonds . . ."

I have to admit a certain input from my own unconscious. Somewhere along the line, I discovered that nothing tastes really bad if you put enough sour cream on it. Hoyt Alden, I told you not to read this.

I did up the artichokes. Paul said he knew there was a reason that he hadn't been voting Republican.

Well, that's my contribution to the Food Pages. There won't be another.

Oh yes, I guess I should add that it's not the first time I've ever dreamed of solutions to pesky food problems. Once in my working/commuting/mothering/cooking days, I dreamed that scientific research has just proved that the dietary secret to health and longevity was an exclusive diet of bread and butter grilled to a golden brown on the outdoor barbecue.

Paul didn't think very much of that dream, either.

TO THE QUEEN

October 3, 1977

Paul and I are beekeepers in a part of the Ozarks where most farmers raise cattle and hogs. They hunker down at the feed store and talk scours and hog lice. We fret about the foul brood and nosema. They are out there castrating calves and cropping pigs' tails. We are inside clipping queens' wings. They wear standard bib overalls and are amused to see us in our white coveralls, gauntlets, and bee veils. They think we are odd, perhaps even unhinged, to make a living raising insects.

We can't keep more than ten hives of bees at any one place because more than that crowds the available bee forage, so we place our hives in outyards rented at a cost of a gallon of honey from farmers who have good stands of clover in their pastures. When they see us drive in to tend our hives, they often come over and banter in a good-natured way or tell us about their grandfathers, all of whom seemed to have robbed bee trees. But they have no real understanding of what it is that we are up to.

131

It was, therefore, a pleasing prospect when a friend told us about old Mr. Fred when we were looking for new bee pasture to place some hives that we had just bought last year. Not only did Mr. Fred have good stands of clover, but he had kept a few hives of bees himself a number of years ago and would be able to understand our problems. "One thing," our friend cautioned, "don't let him get started on the evils of drinking. He's a teetotaler, and once he begins on the subject, he won't let you go for a couple of hours."

We drove over to Mr. Fred's place. It looked like a good location for bees, and he was eager to have them there. We picked out a secluded spot in back of his house and used a grub hoe to flatten out a place to put our hives.

We noticed that he was watching us from his curtained picture window. We were hot and sweaty by the time we drove back down his driveway. He was waiting for us at his side door and called out, "Don't you want to come in and have a drink?"

Paul and I looked at each other, startled. Our friend must have been kidding us. We seldom drink, but we like to remain on friendly terms with people from whom we rent bee pasture, so we followed Mr. Fred into his house. He handed us two glasses of cold water that we swallowed gratefully.

"Yes sir," he said firmly, "water's the stuff. Liquor means ruin. And don't you ever forget it. Why I have a nephew, name of Fred, too, and he was a fine

132

upstanding young man, steady job, beautiful wife, nice home, until he started drinking. . . ."

"Hear you used to be a beekeeper," Paul interrupted, because we could see that Mr. Fred was settling into a comfortable position and warming to his story. Our friend had been right.

"Yep," he replied. "Started keeping bees back in 1912 and there's nothing I can't tell you about bees. No, I guess not." We were pleased. Beekeeping is a complex art and we have always picked up useful information from experienced beekeepers. "I know, for instance," Mr. Fred went on, "that you are making a big mistake putting your bees in that spot you chose out yonder."

We puzzled over that. We had selected a place with shade, protected from the north wind, near a pond. What could have been better?

"I've got a sixth sense about bees," he explained, "and they just won't like it out there." Well, we couldn't argue with a man's sixth sense, but we had spent a lot of time with grub hoes leveling a site that looked good to us, so we decided to stick with it and moved the bees in there a few nights later.

As the spring progressed, we visited the beeyards more frequently and Mr. Fred detailed all the mistakes that we were making each time we visited his place. We could feel his eyes watching us through his window every time we worked there. As we left, he would always come shuffling out in his carpet slippers to comment on our ineptitude.

We divided some of our strong colonies in two.

We did it the wrong way, he said. Even his drunken nephew could have done it better. We put new queens in the hives all wrong. The moon was in a bad phase for that kind of work. When the nectar began to flow in the flowers in the late spring, we started putting on supers—those boxes on tops of the hives that bees fill with honey that would be our crop for the year.

"You're making a big mistake," he told us the day that we drove up to his place with our pickup full of empty supers. "Those bees want a bit of crowding yet. Don't put the supers on too soon." It was a bountiful season and in no time the supers were filled with white wax–capped honey. We kept piling on more supers to Mr. Fred's constant disapproval.

Toward the end of the nectar flow, we drove out of his driveway one day to find him waiting for us as usual. We could pretty well anticipate his opening remark. "You've made a big mistake. You aren't going to be able to get all that honey extracted." Having too much honey was a problem that hadn't occurred to us. The idea amused me, but I could see Paul's jaw tighten. There seemed to be no way to please Mr. Fred.

The honey season is over here by August, so at the beginning of that month we took the heavy supers from the hives and began extracting the honey from them. Extracting honey is a sticky and tiring job, but within two weeks we were done and had a bumper crop of honey. Nature had been kind to us and our hard work had paid off. We took Mr. Fred his gallon of honey for rent and told him happily of our big yield. "You'll never be able to sell it all," he grumbled, "and then you'll have all that honey on your hands."

After most of our honey was sold, we finished up our fall bee chores. We went around to each outyard to check the hives to see that the bees had enough honey stored for the winter, that they were free of disease and most importantly that each hive had a queen in it.

Finding the queen bee in a hive with sixty thousand bees in it is not a simple task. It requires taking out every frame and looking among the crawling worker bees and remaining drones for the queen with her distinctive shape and gait. We usually do it together, four eyes being more helpful than two because it is so easy to overlook the queen in the mass of bees.

We were working our way through our beeyards. Mr. Fred's yard came due and although we had come to dread going there, I noticed that Paul seemed unusually cheerful. As we drove in he said, "It's been a good year and I think that we should celebrate the honey harvest." From a sack he took two wine glasses and a bottle of sherry. He carried them over to the hives while I unloaded from the truck the equipment that we needed to check the hives. He put the bottle and glasses down on hive Number 2 while I started to take apart hive Number 1. I saw the curtains part slightly at Mr. Fred's picture window.

Hive Number 1 was in good shape. It was a healthy colony and had plenty of honey stored to see the bees through the winter, but we had some trouble finding the queen and had to take out nearly every frame before we spotted her. We finally saw her and Paul reached for the sherry and poured each of the glasses half full.

"To the queen," he toasted.

"To the queen," I responded. It looked as though it would be a good afternoon.

Hive Number 2 was in good shape, too, and we found the queen on the second frame we pulled out. I noticed Mr. Fred in the window watching closely.

"To the queen," we cried in unison, quaffing our sherry.

Hive Number 3 was a little low on stores, so we fed it some sugar syrup, found the queen and toasted her. Without really turning my head I could see Mr. Fred at the window. His mouth was slightly open.

We drank to the rest of the queens, too. When we got to hive Number 9, Paul and I had a slight difference of opinion as to whether what I said was a queen might not be a drone, but we soon agreed that it was the queen and a fine old queen she was, certainly deserving a tribute.

We were feeling pleasant toward the world in general when we closed up hive Number 10. We were even feeling friendly toward old Mr. Fred. I noticed that his curtains were completely drawn. We would have toasted him if he had come out of his side door when we drove away. But we never saw him.

THE ENVIRONMENT, FACTORY MODEL

October 28, 1977

I worried a lot when I was a kid.

Would my mother pick me up after school when she said she was going to? Would my brother jump out from behind a door and punch me if I walked into the next room? Would I strangle if I swallowed those stringy home-canned peaches? What would happen to me if I forgot my piece at the piano recital? Who made God? Would I grow up if I never learned to tell time? Did my brother really mean it when he said he'd break my arm the next time he said "Curiosity killed the cat," if I answered "But satisfaction brought him back"? Was there something scary behind the furnace?

In addition to all those more or less transient worries, there were two constant stews that I lived with. I read Coleridge and was afraid that I would become an addict someday and that when I grew up I'd have to write humorous columns for a newspaper. More given to fretting than gay spontaneous creativity, I could never figure out how anyone could think up enough stuff to write about regularly.

My first worry was justified. I simply can't get started in the morning without coffee and just look at the price. But my second worry was groundless. The material for columns accumulates faster than I can write them.

I have a big pasteboard box in which I toss newspaper clippings, scraps of sentences, snippets of overheard conversations, and notes on private idiocies.

Just take a look over my shoulder.

Item: Here's a clipping about a Pole who successfully hijacked a Polish airliner to Vienna, armed only with a piece of rye bread. That could put an end to all those vile ethnic jokes.

Item: This one is an advertisement I received in the mail for a $700 Yoga Health Wheel, a machine that "enables you to achieve the different positions of yoga." End tiresome effort and exertion. Impress your friends by doing a mechanical headstand.

Item: Here's a note that some day I really must write about the outdoor waiting room at the town Airport. Very well, I shall. The outdoor waiting room at the airport is a concrete slab next to the landing strip. Those whose feet grow tired waiting for a flight on the next crop duster may sit on one of the church pews that are arranged in long rows on it. The pews, complete with hymnal racks, were scrounged, no doubt, from a church going-out-of-business-sale, representing Ozark recycling at its best.

I mean the material just keeps piling up. Soon I'm

going to need two boxes for the Human Condition.

But my real favorite in the box is the report of a publicity conference called by a bathroom supply company that shall remain nameless.

It's old-fashioned and unstylish to even consider going into a bathroom just to take a bath when you are dirty, according to the president of the company, who explained, "In today's fast changing world there is a need for solitude and the tranquility and regeneration only nature provides." The trouble is, for one reason or another, there doesn't seem to be enough nature to go around. "Nowhere in the home has there been a place where a person could find this total rest and rejuvenation," he adds, considering going to bed too time-consuming.

Fortunately, the folks at his factory have come up with a solution to this problem in the form of a bathroom unit called The Environment. The Environment is a seven-by-three-foot fiberglass box with cedar floors, teak walls, glass doors, twenty-four-carat gold rain spigots, and an optional stereo.

Inside you can, by punching "an LED digital read-out control panel," make . . . um . . . weather with names like "Baja Sun," "Jungle Steam," or "Chinook Winds" and have "the caress of spring rain," "the gentle buffet of winds," "the pounding of desert sun," all accompanied by a stereo playing soft violin music, or if suitable, thunderclaps.

You and I have tacky old faucets for Hot and Cold. But The Environment has a button for Warm Ambient.

The price of this wonderful weather box is $9900 without the stereo.

It's a delight to read about The Environment. It explains the nagging unease that I have about our Ozark weather that is altogether too haphazard, too excessive, too natural to give us that total relaxation the plumber was talking about. If it's dry we worry about the garden; too much rain and we start to fret about the bees not getting out to make honey; snow and cold makes us wonder if we have enough firewood; too hot and all we can do is sit around in lawn chairs under the oak trees and fan ourselves.

For just $9900 we could go inside the house, shut the doors and windows forever, and trivialize the weather, playing climate and violin music until the end of our days.

Of course with our luck with mechanical gadgets, some vital nut or bolt would drop out of our Environment and we'd be stuck with Chinook Winds howling out of the bathroom and thunderclaps every time we wanted to brush our teeth.

You see? Once a worrier, always a worrier.

KEEP YOUR DAMN
PAPERCLIPS

———

November 15, 1977

When I was in college back in the early fifties, I knew a girl who was engaged to a fledgling psychiatrist. She planned to become a psychiatrist, too, even though medical school and the specialization required would take twelve years. She didn't want to work as a psychiatrist because it was the fifties and she wanted to be a Good Little Wife, but, she said, she wanted to have something in common to talk about with her husband at breakfast. "When the attraction wore off," she added, with a dab of cynicism glinting through the stars in her eyes.

I thought of her occasionally after I married. Paul was a university professor of engineering in those days and I was a librarian at a different university. Over breakfast, he might assure me that Maxwell's Equations were bonny, or at the end of a working day, I might try to entertain him with a particularly delightful Dewey Decimal Number. But there it was, we had no professional interests in common.

When we retired to become farmers and beekeepers in the Ozarks, great waves of harmony washed over us. We were going to do everything together, share our work and problems at breakfast, lunch, and dinner. Different jobs aside, hadn't we always been wonderfully compatible? After twenty years of marriage, we still held hands. We both liked the bedroom window open at night, laughed at Woody Allen, detested boiled cabbage. Why we were as alike as two spines on a cactus.

Compatible?

I didn't even know the guy.

In the twenty-five years we'd been acquainted, he'd never let on that he was a hard-liner on tomato stakes. He prefers straight single stakes and I favor them in groups of three, tepee fashion. Our first June in the Ozarks, we stood out in the garden, sweat streaming down our faces, driving in tomato stakes and trading insults about each other's lineage. At lunch, I kept my lips primly closed. There didn't seem to be much to say to a man whose outlook on the world was so vastly different from mine.

When we simplified our lives and sold our house and most of the things that filled it, we reasoned that we didn't need separate desks. One desk was plenty for two loving retired people who were going to keep some bees and grow a few tomatoes. Neither of us would say "my desk" anymore; we'd say "our desk."

He likes scraps of paper with addresses on the top of the desk where he can keep an eye on them, mingled with old receipts, piles of dusty pennies, canceled checks, and rusted bolts from the lawn mower. When I sit down at the desk, I file, put things in little heaps, and arrange them, hoping that the act of tidying will order the clutter in my mind.

He says I hide things.

After a lively morning spent doing the income tax together, I moved *my* typing paper, *my* paper clips, and *my* envelopes up to a card table in the barn loft. It was hard to carry that off with the dignity required because there are no stairs going up to the loft, just an old ladder with a couple of rungs missing. But after I got everything up there, I pulled the ladder up behind me and slammed shut the door, a second-hand door that we bought at an auction, bearing, appropriately, a sign that says NO ADMITTANCE. Unfortunately the sign is on the inside of the door.

There is, of course, much work to share.

I picked up a bit of mechanics so that we could work on machinery together and being an indifferent and uninterested cook, I was delighted when Paul decided to learn cookery so that we could share that chore, too. He settled down one afternoon in the brown leather chair with a stack of cookbooks and asked me to stick around so that I could answer questions.

"How many teaspoons to a tablespoon," he began. "What does it mean cook until thickened? How thick? Bake until done. Now what does that mean? No one would write a Chevy manual like this. What does cream of tartar do? Why use a wooden spoon for stirring? Do we have a Bundt pan? Where are the toasted almonds? How can you just leave things out when the recipe says to put them in? How do you braise? How does yeast work? How do you expect me to make paella without saffron?"

"I don't know. I don't care. Leave it out. I forget. Perfectionist," I shrieked.

Of course beekeeping is different. It was a new skill for both of us. We read books together, talked to experts together, watched beekeepers together. We noted with detached amusement that every beekeeper develops fierce, fanatical opinions on beekeeping and, coordinately, a very low regard for the opinions of other beekeepers. But not us. No, we work side by side, bee smoker to bee smoker, mind to mind.

When we work in our outyards, we pack a picnic lunch in a wicker hamper, a cold chicken, a bottle of white wine, some fruit, just a modest lunch for retired folks. Over those business lunches we hold hands and discuss new labels for our honey jars, beekeeping problems, the weather, and the nectar flow.

Take the other day, for example. In the morning we had been working in our outyards. At midday, we spread out our lunch on a checkered tablecloth beside an Ozark stream in the shade of some sycamore trees. As he flicked an ant off our cloth, Paul mentioned that we needed to clean out the crystallized honey from the bottom of one of the one hundred gallon storage tanks in the honey house. I took a piece of chicken and said, yes, we could carry the tank outdoors, open it up, and let the bees clean it out.

"Can't do that," Paul said, pulling the cork out of

the wine bottle with his teeth. Silly me. I'd forgotten the corkscrew again. "The bees will get all excited and start robbing each other's hives."

"Not if we put the tank more than five hundred feet from the hives," I said, warming to my point of view and beginning a thoughtful, well-reasoned lecture on the function of distance in the bee dance and the dance as a means of communicating food sources to honey bees, a perfectly delightful and jolly little lecture.

Paul interrupted. "Everyone who writes for beekeeping magazines says not to encourage robbing by feeding out old honey like that." He keeps very up-to-date in his reading.

"Well, *I* write for the beekeeping magazines," I said airily, reminding him of the check I had just received that morning from a beekeeping magazine for as harmless and innocent a screed as was ever perpetrated upon an editor, "and so if I say it, it's true."

He looked at me in disgust. His ears were just a little red.

"All right, all right. You find me *one* place, just *one* place where it says in print that it is OK to let bees clean up a honey tank and start a lot of robbing and all . . ."

His voice trailed off and he looked at me suspiciously. I was taking notes.

I wonder if my friend ever became a psychiatrist. Do she and her husband dissect neuroses over dinner? After all that was the fifties. "Grease" notwithstanding, who wants the fifties with its loyalty oaths, sack dresses, conversation pits, McCarthyism, Nice Girls, and Togetherness. Who needs Togetherness?

Hey, Paul, it really is OK to let bees clean out honey from storage tanks.

LONG ISLAND
INTERLUDE

February 3, 1978

We are in New York for the winter, amassing enough money to support our bees in the style to which they have become accustomed.

It won't come as any surprise to St. Louisans, I suppose, if I point out that the weather last year left something to be desired. It reduced the bees' honey production at our place in the Ozarks and that was hard on us financially because we had chosen last year to expand our honey operations from a cottage industry to an agribusiness.

So, Paul and I are working this winter.

Perhaps I'm just accustomed to the peace and quiet down in the hills, but it seems like there is a lot happening here. Right after we arrived, an oil tanker ran aground and spilled its cargo along the beaches. The Coast Guard never did get it all cleaned up because of a bad sleet storm that covered everything with a thick layer of ice.

The wind blew hard and broke down icy trees and

power lines, leaving 400,000 persons out here on Long Island without power for most of a week. After a bit of a thaw, there was a big fire in the center of Huntington where we are living. Half a dozen shops burned to the ground and the smoke damaged many others. The next day a nor'easter raged through, leaving two feet of snow in its wake, and downed more power lines. The governor declared an emergency and sent in the National Guard. Few of the guardsmen knew how to repair power lines, so they stood around, smiling sheepishly and stamping their feet to keep warm.

Benevolent organizations flew into action, doling out hot chocolate, soup, blankets, and directions on how to preserve tropical fish in homes without power and heat.

The trains stopped. The banks closed. The expressways were closed down and everyone started talking to everyone else. That is a real emergency for New Yorkers.

I don't know what New York is going to do next, but it has caught my attention.

We've just moved into an apartment. It's OK, but I miss my beagle badly. He and the other dogs, the cats, the chickens, and all the dormant bees are staying home on the farm with a young couple who are living there and looking after the place for us. They promised to do all the hardest things like keeping the dog dinner dishes straight and offering chopped corn to the introverted hen who lives under the feed barrel.

I've already figured out how many more weeks it

will be until the bees start flying and I can come back home to Missouri.

It was soothing to ring up the postmaster at home the other day and to hear him tell me in his slow drawl that he would forward our mail. In the Ozarks, our *Post-Dispatch* comes in the mail one day late, our *New York Times* two days after that. Radio news is beamed at us from Rolla over National Public Radio, which reports everything in a temperate sort of way. I'm not really sure I want to buy a fresh newspaper here and read the news so immediately. It's easier on the nerves to get it as history.

I keep the Ozarks in mind because life there seems more reasonable and calmer.

I'd forgotten how quick New York speech is. I keep asking people to repeat what they say because I can't keep up with them.

I suffered a real case of cultural shock once, nearly twenty years ago, when we went to France and discovered that they spoke French there. We were graduate students in those days and had scraped together enough money to spend the summer camping in Europe. I possessed, supposedly, a modicum of French, so I had volunteered to talk to people while we were in France.

We arrived in Paris without a hotel reservation and I wandered about trying to find a meal and lodging for Paul, Brian, and myself for the first night. I was horrified to realize that my painstakingly formulated questions weren't enough. There were replies. Those Parisians, once they suffered the indignity that I was

inflicting upon their language, answered me in French
and I couldn't understand a word they said.

By mistake, I wandered into a bar with the same
name as a hotel that we were looking for and carefully, Frenchily, precisely, asked the man in charge if
he had a bed for the night.

With a lewd grin and a Gallic bow, he replied, "A
votre service, madame."

Blushing furiously, I ran out of the bar and collapsed into a little heap of inutility, having for the first
time, understood a Frenchman's reply.

Somehow, with hand signs and his charming
smile, Paul got us a room for the night and the next
day we went over to the park in the center of Paris,
the Bois de Boulogne, and set up our tent. I crawled
into it, sick with anxiety and a migraine headache, and
refused to come out for a week. Paul and Brian,
smiling, gesturing, and pointing at passages in a phrase
book, had a fine time in Paris. Eventually I crept out
of the tent and started enjoying myself, too.

Of course, New York isn't all that foreign, but it
is different. People aren't really irritated here, but they
are preoccupied and sometimes they act that way.
Everyone is hustling. No one is what he seems to be.

The real estate man who found our apartment
mostly thought about his potato futures.

The dental technicians who cleaned my teeth the
other day said she was "into fleas," which didn't mean
that she trained those insects for a side show, but that
she bought and sold things. She confided that she was
working on a deal in airplanes and hoped to make a
$100,000 commission. Honest, that's what she said.

She was also "into" bloodworms, reincarnation, bingo, and astrology. I wish her good luck.

A waitress advised me that the only way to get ahead in an office is to set up a personal company and subcontract all the office business to it.

I've met a magician.

A taxicab driver that I rode with told me that he really was the czar of the hot roofing compound industry.

An accountant told me that nearly everyone in his office is in the numbers racket and that the whole company was crawling with undercover agents dressed in Mother Hubbards and posing as cleaning ladies.

Psssst! Eat this page of the newspaper after you've finished reading it.

I'm steering clear of any hustles and have passed up an invitation to join a Transcendental Meditation group that is learning to levitate. I'm keeping it firmly in mind that we're just a pair of beekeepers with a cash flow problem.

Actually, we are settling in and having a pretty good time. We've seen a lot of movies, enjoyed several musical evenings, and visited a number of old friends. I've spent several pleasant days in an agricultural library reading up on bees and several more rummaging through book stores.

If the winter ever loosens its grip on the Long Island Railroad and lets the trains roll, I'll head into Manhattan and start memorizing subway lines.

I'll keep you posted.

Going Home

March 21, 1978

"St. Louis is a big city," I told the travel agent.

"I've heard that," he said politely, but mulishly continued to insist that bus transportation out of St. Louis, if it existed at all, would be available on only the most primitive basis.

"Buses, trains, airplanes, lots of things go in and out of St. Louis all the time," I told him. "It's where the wagons stock up with victuals and provisions for the long trip West."

He was not amused.

I am coming back to the Ozarks before Paul, who is keeping the van, so I needed a combination of reservations on an airplane and several buses. The only bus that ever goes to the town I call home leaves Rolla at six in the morning and so my airplane reservation depended on what time I could get a connecting bus from St. Louis to arrive in Rolla at dawn.

A succession of travel agents had found this an impossible challenge. They told me that bus schedules

152

were all printed with New York as the navel of the universe and that there was no way to find out about a St. Louis bus if, indeed, there was such a thing. This last agent tried to talk to a computer about travel in the Heartland. The computer suggested that I might enjoy taking a bus from St. Louis to somewhere it (and then the agent) insisted on calling Polar Bluff and then going home, a 250-mile, twelve-hour detour.

"Wrong, wrong, wrong!" I said, but the computer just sat there in smug silence.

Eventually I took matters in my own hands, rang up the bus station in Rolla, and made my own airline reservation. I was properly thankful that I wasn't planning a trip through Africa with a New York travel agent. The agent called me a few days later and tried to interest me in a special flight to Miami with a bus tour of the Everglades.

"I don't want to go to Florida," I told him. "I want to go home." And I do.

It will be good to be back in the Ozarks again.

Long Island, where we are living, is perhaps best appreciated by regarding its architectural specialties, the Diner, and the Catering Palace.

The standard Jersey diner, that eatery of chrome and Formica, has evolved rankly and luxuriantly here. Chrome and Formica are still visible under the demented, heavy opulence of red, tasseled velvet drapes, flocked wallpaper, and colonial pillars. There is food, of a kind, in them too. They are perfect Disneylands of the palate, the carbohydrate capitals of the world. The mirrored shelves multiply the mounds of ornate, garish, billowing pastries, stuffed with fruit that never was and chemical cream.

But the quintessence of Long Island rococo is its catering establishments. There are thirteen pages of caterers listed in the Nassau Yellow Pages. They are not simple businesses that will send over a few canapés for a party. No, indeed. They are, rather, complete, stagish, overdone, overblown party houses that can be rented out as a facade for celebrations where men in powder-blue tuxedos escort women who spend their other waking hours redistributing wealth in shopping malls. The catering palaces flaunt themselves along the highways, perfect frenzies of white wrought iron, imitation crystal chandeliers, and plastic luxury.

There is, incidentally, a place in the town where we live where you can rent plastic flowers.

I'd like to set loose a Martian anthropologist out here.

I've enjoyed New York City and even mastered the subways a bit. My use of the Seventh Avenue IRT is rated fair to good by my friends, although they all say I need work on other lines.

I went over to Brooklyn on the subway from midtown Manhattan the other evening for dinner with friends. At 10:15, I got ready to catch a subway back to the railroad station for my ride home.

"I don't mean to be provincial," I said, "but is this safe? I mean, I read such dreadful stories in the newspapers . . ."

"Perfectly safe," one of my friends said and then began entertaining me with all the scary things that happen on that subway line. He told me that they had returned from a party just the week before and had been threatened by a group of burly teenagers with bicycle chains. One of the young bullies had an open gash in his cheek, received in a recent brawl.

"And there were two of you," I pointed out, "and you're going to put just one of me on that very subway."

"Oh, it's OK," he said, "that sort of thing doesn't start to happen until at least an hour from now."

When I got on the subway, I chose a seat next to an enormously sturdy woman, deciding that if she had an ounce of charity, I would become a muggee only over her dead body.

I arrived home, not mugged or raped at all and insufferably proud of myself.

Music report: A mixed bag last week. Laser Rock at the Planetarium and a harpsichord recital. The harpsichordist, Kenneth Cooper, who played on a 1784 instrument, was good in the first part of the program as he played Scarlatti, Bach, and Handel. After the intermission, he was astounding. He returned to the keyboard, jacketless, in a vibrant pink and orange ruffled shirt with a red bow tie and settled down to play rags—mostly by Missouri's own Scott Joplin, but with a triumphant "Washington Post March" as a finale. The audience loved it. I guess you've just never heard the harpsichord until you've heard ragtime played on it.

But now all that is past. My work at the New York Public Library is done. I've checked out the last

Libyan motif at the Metropolitan Museum of Art. I must turn my thoughts to bees and springtime in the hills.

I do hope those buses are still running out of St. Louis.

FACTORY WOMEN

_1977_

For the past twenty-five years, factory owners have been moving their plants out of the Northeast and away from established industrial cities, setting up assembly lines in the South and in small towns where they have found cheap and steady labor. The factory owners have been interested in costs, but life is full of surprises, and by hiring workers, many of them women, who have never worked for wages before, they have changed life in rural America. The changes are so radical that today factory owners are puzzled by the new society they have helped to create.

According to a local wit, when the factories moved into the Ozark hills, they created a new class of men whom he calls the "Real Go-Getters." They are the men who drive their wives to work in the factories and then hunker down for the rest of the day until it's time to "go get 'er."

Most Ozark men are not Real Go-Getters and disapprove of those who are, holding that the Go-

Getters should not hunker down, but should work a cash crop, raise pigs, or cut cordwood for a living. But most of them think that it is good for the women to be able to work in the factories for cash money, provided, of course, that they keep up with the home chores and are responsible for the children.

The factories pay low, piecework wages for mind-numbing, repetitive work, offer few fringe benefits, seldom promote women, and throw a fine picnic every year. Yet they have put money into women's hands and are working a social revolution.

Apparel manufacturers, including H. D. Lee Company, Angelica Uniform Company, and Barad & Company, all have factories in the Ozark hills of south central Missouri. Shoe manufacturers, such as Conaway-Winter, Inc., Brown Shoe Company, and International Shoe Company, are here, too. All of them advertise that they will hire both men and women as sewing machine operators, but sewing is women's work so few men apply or are hired.

Angelica and Conaway-Winter both have plants in my town. It is a village of 1,320 people, in some of the prettiest country in the Ozarks.

In days past it was the center of a timber products industry, but most of the trees have been cut now and the land cleared to raise cattle and hogs. A few small wood products factories survive and hire men to work in them, but the women in the industrial work force outnumber the men 246 to 142.

The community is part of a fragile, quiet America, not reflected in newspaper headlines. There are no fast-food franchises here, no shopping centers. Life is savored a bit, friendliness is genuine, manners gracious, speech slow, but the wit sharp ("Supposed to rain today. 'Course I just heard that on one of them little bitty cheap radios, so's it may not be true"). The sign in front of the town hall proclaiming the village name is a painted over Pepsi-Cola sign in the shape of a four-foot bottle cap. Ozarkers were recycling long before it was chic to do so.

Heavy drugs and heavy crime are not a part of the picture. There are eleven churches in the town with well-attended Sunday services, Bible Study Classes, Prayer Meetings, and Wednesday Night Sings. It is a town that gives its conservative congressman, Richard Ichord, overwhelming support in election after election.

Townsfolk and farmers alike get up early in the morning. The factories begin work at 7:30 and many of the stores open then, also. People taper off early in the afternoon, too. The stores close by five and folks go home, eat supper, and go to bed. Houses are dark in the evenings and the streets are quiet and empty save for a few teenagers who cruise the darkened three-block downtown in a desultory way, occasionally stopping in groups of three and four to lounge on the hoods of their cars, waiting vainly, but patiently, for something to happen.

Ozark women have always deferred to their menfolk for all the usual reasons, but also because heavy farm work and the big families needed to do that work haven't allowed much latitude for fancy social experiments. Women have been reluctant to speak out on community affairs and have a dismal voting record.

"Never voted in my life," says a seventy-year-old farm woman. "But *he* does, *he* votes some," she adds as Ozark women do, using the male pronoun rather than his name to refer to their husbands.

Ozark women have not felt easy behind the wheel of the family pickup, that symbol of masculinity in the hills. In a place where there is no public transportation, not even taxis, a woman who can't drive must be taken to town to buy a spool of thread, driven to work if she has a job, must ask for a ride to visit a friend. A woman's place has been sitting on the passenger's side of the pickup and when her husband stops to visit a crony, she should not get out and kick the tires or talk over the points of a closed drive shaft as he does.

And today there are still women in the Ozarks like Sarah. Sarah lives alone back in the hills on a small farm. Her house is cheerful with crisp curtains and windows full of plants potted in old coffee cans. Sarah has never worked for cash money. She sells a few eggs and some milk from her cow. She eats what her garden produces and slaughters a pig now and then. That's heavy work, but she is used to it. Even when her husband was alive, Sarah did most of the farm work while he tinkered with the pickup. She never learned to drive it, but sometimes her husband would take her into town on Saturdays when all the farm people go there to shop. He died a few years ago, but the pickup still stands in the barn. There is a piece of clean cloth over the windshield and hood to keep it nice.

"I couldn't sell it," Sarah says quietly. "*He* wouldn't have wanted me to."

The Angelica Uniform Company, which in our town makes mostly uniform jackets, opened its first factory here back in 1949. Several hundred women were interviewed for jobs. Fifteen were hired and thirteen showed up for work the first day. Among them was Myrtle Glass, who says that she, like the others, was scared. Most of them had never worked for wages before and didn't know if they'd be able to do factory work. Many did not come back the second day. But Myrtle was determined to work for Angelica. As a child she had been moved from school to school because of her father's timbering job. She remembers the heartache the moves caused her, and she wanted to raise her own four children in one place. Her husband had opened a feed mill in town and Angelica offered her a way to make money, the only way if she was to stay here. A skilled home sewer, she learned how to operate all the different sewing machines and within a few months she was promoted to supervisor, later assistant plant manager. A few years later, she was made manager of the factory with one hundred employees working for her. In 1967 the factory moved to a bigger, modern building south of town and Myrtle Glass went on to manage the Angelica plant in a small town nearby.

Myrtle's promotions were typical in Angelica's

early days in the Ozarks, but not today. There are no women managers at the local plant where the regional headquarters are. Women, who despite their age are always called "girls," have a right to apply for any job to which their seniority and education entitles them, but the women who work in the factory are convinced, whether it is true or not, that women will no longer be considered seriously for management jobs. Although Lewis Medlin, recently hired from an Arkansas apparel factory as Angelica's regional personnel director, denies it, the women say that it is now unacknowledged company policy to replace even the women assembly line supervisors with men (who are never called "boys") as those positions become open. Many women excuse this policy by saying that men are better at supervising women than other women are, and that men can travel and be transferred more easily than married women.

However, Myrtle Glass worked almost all of her years at Angelica in either a supervisory or managerial job and thinks that women can do the work. She is a self-assured woman and proud of her work with Angelica. She is proud that her salary helped build the comfortable air-conditioned house that she and her husband live in today. She says that other women working for Angelica have contributed to family well-being. A recent survey of Angelica employees showed that 60 percent of the women working there earned more than half of their family's income.

Myrtle speaks of the changes she observed in her twenty years at Angelica. She tells of the women who had to be driven to work by their husbands, who, she adds scornfully, sometimes had no jobs themselves. Most of those women learned to drive and bought their own cars. She speaks of women who first came to work looking as though they had given up on themselves, graceless, awkward, shy, shabbily dressed, discouraged, who later began to stand tall and dress stylishly. Angelica, she believes, helped women recognize their worth and strength.

Myrtle retired in 1969 and today teaches a Vocational Education Class at the high school, a part-time job that she regards as a community service. Each year she trains a dozen senior girls to sew on industrial sewing machines donated by Conaway-Winter and Angelica. She tries to teach work habits and attitudes that she developed over twenty years, but most of the graduates move out of the Ozarks to take higher-paying, more interesting jobs in big cities, and few go to work for the local factories. This is a problem for the men who manage Angelica and Conaway-Winter. They wish they could attract and keep younger workers because many of the older, steadier women are retiring and their attitudes, their pride in work, and loyalty to the factories are not easy to replace.

The new Angelica factory in town is well lighted, but windowless. Conveyor belts run the length of the building and move uniform fabric pieces along the assembly lines where the sewing machine operators sit. At present there are 15 men working there and 185 women. Mary Willbanks is one of them. She is an inspector and a hard worker, proved by her hourly piece rate, usually about four dollars an hour, which is a high one in the factory. It is also a high rate for the Ozarks, despite the fact that the national industrial average wage is $5.48 an hour. Sewing machine operators complain that the Angelica rates are "tight." So much sewing is required in each work unit that it is hard for them to do enough of it to "make their time," factory jargon for turning out enough work units at the designated rates to make the federal minimum wage of $2.30 an hour. There is a general uneasiness among the women that if productivity increases or the federal minimum wage goes up, the units of required work will be increased, too, and add to the pressure that many of them already feel.

Mary Willbanks has worked for Angelica for twenty-four years and spent fifteen of them as president of the local chapter of the union, the United Garment Workers. UGW organized the plant, a closed shop, in 1956 after a battle with the International Ladies Garment Workers, a union with a more aggressive reputation than the UGW. Mary is now vice president of the local and says that it is hard to get young women interested in union affairs. She is proud of her work with the union, but does not think that the UGW and Angelica, which is earning record profits, are adversaries. She believes that the two work together to protect and create jobs. Workers at Angelica in town have never struck, but Mary herself called a slowdown recently. On one hot day the air conditioning had been turned on for the offices, but not the factory. "Girls, turn off your belts," she says she told the sewing machine operators. "And, you know? They *did*," she adds, pleased. The conveyor belts were off for fifteen minutes until the air conditioning came on in the factory. Mary Willbanks, like other older workers, is very loyal to Angelica and, despite her work with the union, defends most management decisions. She has been offered other jobs in stores in town, but has turned them down because she thinks Angelica is the best place to work. She says she even misses going to work when the plant closes down for two weeks in the summer. People who have worked for Angelica for more than four years are paid at their average quarterly piecework rate for those two weeks, but others who have not worked so long receive only partial payment.

Mary Willbanks and other older women workers can remember the 1930s and the hard times. They think that it is a privilege to have a job and a regular paycheck and they don't mind that Angelica doesn't offer fringe benefits such as paid sick leave or a retirement program. They enjoy working with other women, most of whom have become close friends. The company potlucks, Thanksgiving parties, and picnics are important to them, too. Women, many of whom live on isolated farms, talk of working with other women as though they were taking part in a giant consciousness-raising session. They talk of friendship, learning how other women think, discovering that their cares and worries are shared by other women. They also like Angelica's air conditioning and generally pleasant working conditions, the break area with vending machines and a microwave oven which Lewis Medlin, director of Personnel, just had installed.

Younger women, growing up in a more prosperous America, have a higher set of expectations than their mothers, partly because they have been raised by mothers who worked in the factories. The younger women puzzle the older workers and exasperate the factory personnel men who can't understand why the old methods of making employees happy, productive, and loyal are no longer working. The young women are not proud of their jobs. They take the working conditions for granted. Their friends are outside the factory. They are less serious about the work and think that the pay is low. One young woman showed her paycheck as proof—after deductions it came to seventy-four dollars for a week's work. Young women resent being hired as only a pair of eyes and hands. They complain of the fatigue of sitting in one position all day long. They are not as loyal as the older workers and often quit in irritation or boredom. One young mother hired to sew collars said that at the end of two weeks she was either going to cry or smash the sewing machine, so she quit.

"We needed the money," she says, "but there wasn't enough money in the world to make me sew that same collar seam over and over again for the rest of my life."

Younger women are aware of the changing status of women all over the country and they resent being locked into dead-end jobs. They notice ruefully that men hired as mechanics are usually encouraged and promoted, and they know women who have applied for men's jobs, such as Mechanic or Presser, who have been talked into withdrawing their applications. The younger women are unenthusiastic union members and believe that the union is powerless to change the things that they think are wrong in the factories.

One young Angelica employee says that she wants to stay in the Ozarks because her husband likes farming here, but she doesn't know how much longer she can stand working at Angelica.

She operates an automatic sewing machine that barely requires watching and so she spends a lot of time thinking about what is going on around her. The factory, she observes, has no windows and she wonders if maybe that is why the women who work there seem to be so involved with themselves and their small circle of factory friends. She thinks that their jobs help only themselves and she would like to help other people with her life. Asked if there was any way she would want to go on working for Angelica, she replies that if she thought she could be promoted to some job like Personnel or Quality Control, she would like to stay, but adds that a woman sewing machine operator would never be promoted to jobs like those.

She also says that she grew up angry. She never understood her anger until just recently when she realized that her family and people around her had always pushed her to do things considered to be feminine. Her father, she remembers, would never show her how to repair the pickup, but would suggest instead that her mother teach her how to sew. Today she sews for a living, but she also knows how to fix her own car. She now understands her own anger, but hasn't yet quite come to terms with it.

"All the way through high school," she says, "we were told to improve ourselves and never settle for anything less than the best." Spending the rest of her days operating an automatic sewing machine is not her idea of the Best in Life and she plans to quit soon and go to college. She'd like to open a few windows on the world. Maybe, she muses, she could become a teacher . . . a woman could do that . . . or perhaps a social worker . . .

In 1954, plagued by problems in trying to create a stable work force in St. Louis, Conaway-Winter moved its manufacturing operations to a nearby Ozark town, Willow Springs, taking part in a trend that has put 42 percent of shoe manufacturing in this country in towns with populations less than five thousand. Shoe manufacturers across the country are in trouble these days from foreign import competition and Conaway-Winter is in even greater trouble because it manufactures children's shoes. Not only is the birth rate down but today parents often put their children in sneakers or let them go barefoot. Nevertheless, Conaway-Winter must be doing something right, because in 1974 it refurbished the old Angelica building in my town and opened a second factory here to produce soft-soled infants' shoes.

When Angelica operated in the building, the women running the sewing machines on hot muggy Missouri summer afternoons would wring out towels in cold water and drape them around their necks and keep on working. Today the stifling summer air is kept moving in the old building by big industrial fans.

The sixty-two workers, fifty-two of them women, turn out 2,500 to 3,000 tiny shoes here each day.

The work, as at Angelica, is broken down into single operations. Each sewer sews the same seam over and over and over again. Each shoe lacer laces and laces and laces again.

Leather is cut into shoe pieces and the like pieces are sorted into wire baskets making up work units. A blue work ticket travels in each basket, which is hand-carried from sewer to sewer. Coupons with work values assigned to each operation are attached to the work ticket. When a woman finishes all the pieces in her basket, she tears off the coupon assigned to her particular seam. The coupons that she collects during the day add up to her pay for that day. If her seam is assigned a work value of 61 cents, she must do nearly four baskets an hour to "make her time," the federal minimum of $2.30 an hour that the company must pay her. If she can't sew that many baskets, she may be fired because the company is losing money on her. But if she can do more, she will make a better wage.

From 7:30 until 4:00 every day, women sit in the old factory building at the heavy black industrial sewing machines, eyes focused intently on the pieces of work bathed in a pool of light. Fingers move swiftly and skillfully because errors are sent back and cut into the pay rate. Motions are quick, smooth, efficient, rhythmic.

Shoe styles change, and sewing machine operators dislike having to learn new stitches. Not only does learning a new procedure slow down the sewer so that her pay rate is lower, but the mind must be focused, the brain put in gear until it trains the fingers. The women prefer to let the eyes and skilled hands repeat and repeat and repeat a familiar motion and let the mind, unglued, wander to interesting thoughts rather than concentrate on a scrap of infants' shoe.

Some Conaway-Winter women have been promoted to supervisory positions as they have been Angelica. President Frank Winter recalls that there was once a woman vice-president and that some women have held management jobs in the past. Today, however, there are few women other than secretaries in the executive offices and no women managers at the local factory.

The plant union, Boot and Shoe Workers of America, first organized the Willow Springs factory fifteen years ago and enjoys a closed shop in both plants. The union has never called a strike, and in a financially unsettled industry, union officials confess that they cannot take an aggressive position. Local union meetings are poorly attended.

Worker loyalty to Conaway-Winter is strong among older women. Even younger workers consider supervisors and managers to be decent, understanding people who do what they can. But finding steady, dedicated younger women to replace the retiring older workers is a problem for Conaway-Winter. Younger women are applying for jobs in fewer numbers and are quitting for much the same reasons as they do at Angelica. Turnover is a serious problem in an industry where it takes at least six months to train an average sewing machine operator who must be paid $2.30 an hour whether she produces that much in piecework or not. Frank Winter no longer recognizes many of the workers as he walks through his factory and he wishes that he understood the young workers well enough to keep that turnover rate down.

The most obvious local impact of having 246 women industrial employees is, of course, economic. According to Frank Winter, each one dollar paid in wages in a factory town is circulated through the local economy ten times. Paychecks that women spend in town keep business doors open.

The two factories pump roughly $1.3 million new dollars into the economy of a town of 1,300 people.

Most of those dollars are in the hands of women who have done hard, tedious work for them. Women factory workers consider the work they do at home—the child care, the vegetable gardening, the canning, housework, cooking, and help with the farm—to be their share of responsibility for the household, so the work that they do in the factories is extra. Therefore they can decide how to spend their wages themselves.

The few women in the factories who turn over their paychecks to their husbands in traditional Ozark wife fashion are scolded by their coworkers.

A local furniture store owner recalled that a factory worker came in one day recently and bought a refrigerator. After she had paid for it, she asked that it be delivered to her home the next day. She would be at work, she explained, but her husband would be there to take it. The delivery men came back to the store the next day, amused, and said that when they delivered the refrigerator, the husband was surprised, didn't know about the refrigerator, didn't want the refrigerator, didn't need the refrigerator, but said he reckoned since his wife had paid for it, he'd better take the damn refrigerator.

"Yep," the furniture store dealer said, "the women are spending their own paychecks and they aren't buying fence posts with it."

He's wrong, of course. Some of them do buy fence posts and help with other farm expenses. Or buy groceries. Or set up small businesses. Or buy antiques. Or help out needy relatives. Or finance vacations. Or buy pretty clothes. Or send their children to college. But they make the decisions.

Women are learning to drive and are buying cars. The village mayor says that more older women are taking drivers' tests. The high school in recent years has offered Drivers' Education and today 100 percent of the sophomore girls sign up for the optional course. The owner of the biggest auto dealership in town believes that half again as many women are driving today as were ten years ago and says that it is because so many women need to drive to work. When a couple comes in to buy a car, he says, he sells to the wife because she is the one who makes the decision and often has the money to pay for it.

A number of bad or dreary marriages have been ended by women factory workers who have discovered that they were financially and emotionally independent. Several women remember the wife who took a factory job to pay off the mortgage on the family farm. Her husband spent most of his days drinking coffee in town at Vance's Leona's Cafe, a name that it is probably not really useful to ponder. The wife raised the children, did the household chores and much of the farm work after her work day at the factory was over. After she had paid off the mortgage and had the farm in her name, she told her husband to leave.

"The factories," says Joan Smith, our new mayor, "have helped give our women some confidence. They have taken their hair out of little buns and cut it. They have traded their shapeless print dresses for pants suits. They have become more independent."

Joan Smith, who had run for mayor before and lost, ran again last year and won. Although she had been involved in community affairs for a number of years and had served on the town council, many people didn't like the idea of having a woman mayor. Surprisingly, much of the opposition came from women themselves, suggesting perhaps that although Ozark women are growing more self-confident, they are not yet confident enough to trust another woman on the basis of her qualifications. Joan Smith says that she won only because she had two male opponents who split the vote. Now that she is mayor, however, she says women who never spoke up are calling her with their problems, letting her know when the garbage truck is late, or that there is a dog running loose. Women are beginning to volunteer to serve on civic committees. Mayor Smith thinks that women are beginning to discover that their opinions are worth something and are voting more. Factory workers say that they talk about the candidates before an election and remind each other to vote.

Up the highway in Houston, Missouri, a woman presides over the county court as judge. More women are to be found managing businesses, working on newspapers, selling insurance, and pumping gas in the Ozarks than in the old days.

The Women's Chamber of Commerce, a group of town women, has become a civic force. It is trying to prod the town into action to make it a better place for young people to live. Right now the WCC is urging the town to build a public swimming pool to provide a summertime gathering place for teenagers. Mayor Smith finds the WCC more energetic than the Chamber of Commerce, which has only male membership. "Sometimes I think that the men in this town are just tired," she says with a smile.

Economic power, mobility, independence, stronger feelings of self-worth, women becoming aware of other women, political involvement—this is the stuff of the Women's Movement across the nation. But, ironically, "Women's Lib," as it is called locally, finds no favor. Women frown at feminist buzzwords like Abortion, Lesbianism, Day Care.

This is not to say that there are no radical feminists to be found in the Ozarks. Among the back-to-the-landers who have been drifting into the hills in recent years, a number of well-educated, urban, verbal women peer at their own cervixes, each with her own speculum, and do other amusing and up-to-date things as well. But their lives are remote from those of the farm women or the women who sit at the sewing machines in the factories. They speak differently, dress differently, and look at the world in a different way. Those differences are more noticeable to the native Ozark women than their common gender and they seldom have much to do with one another.

Probably many of the same people who didn't like the idea of a woman mayor are also opposed to the Equal Rights Amendment, which has been the subject of fiery opposition by Fundamentalist male preachers in the area. The local representative to the state legislature, Wendell Bailey, first voted for the ERA, waffled, and then joined his colleagues in defeating it. This past spring he polled his constituents and found that 80 percent of them are opposed to the ERA. Although the factory workers are emphatically in favor of equal pay for equal work, the older ones say that they don't approve of the ERA because they think that it stands for disruption of family life, the possibility of a woman's draft, and integrated rest rooms.

Mayor Smith, who favors the Equal Rights

Amendment, has been offered support by a coalition of women's groups from St. Louis to run for the state legislature. But she doesn't think that she is ready for that job yet. Maybe she will when the women in the area, already an economic majority, become a more self-confident social and political force.

Certainly there are signs that the women in the Ozarks are beginning to question the rigid social structure that they have lived with in the past. The women who work in the factories are more independent than their mothers. The workers' daughters, who have grown up freer, are looking beyond the factories and planning careers.

These are heady changes and probably not the ones the factory owners had in mind when they moved to the Ozarks. The steady work force is steady no longer. A microwave oven in the break area will not keep young women at Angelica. And a swimming pool will not keep them in town, it being the nature of young people to go look for Something to Happen.

Assembly line production, if it is to continue in towns like this town, will have to be changed to keep any kind of work force at all. And the changes will have to be radical indeed to make much difference to young women who are serving notice to anyone who will bother to listen that they and other women like them in country towns are no longer America's Third World.

THE HONEY WAR

Winter is long and harsh on the prairie. The winds blow down out of the north, running for mile after unobstructed mile, driving snow into drifts around houses, making every human task a struggle. Sometimes men and women go a little mad there in the winter.

The winter of 1839 came early and by the first part of December, the snow was already deep along the Missouri-Iowa border, but on the night of December 15, most of the citizens of Lewis County, in northern Missouri, had braved the snow and cold to meet at Pemberton's Hotel in Monticello, the county seat. They wanted to put on record just how it was they felt about their neighbors—those "foreign bandits"—the residents of the Territory of Iowa, who had "perpetuated a foul indignity upon the escutcheon of our State."

The sheriff from another Missouri county had tried recently to perform his "official duties" in what,

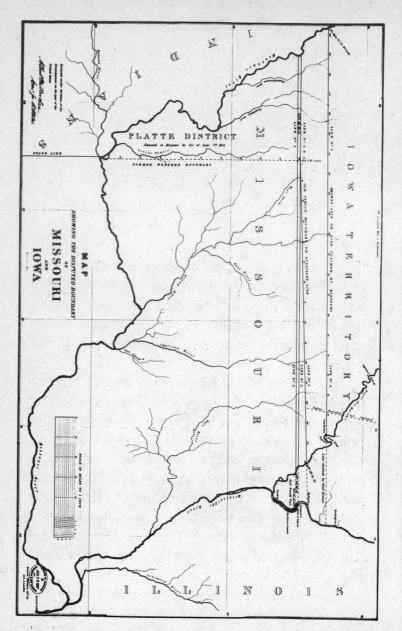

they held, was Missouri and had been "forcibly seized and carried away by a band of lawless depredators," the Iowans, an act that threatened "the supremacy of our laws, the inviolability of our soil."

A hot and windy series of resolutions was passed that evening, including one stating

> That when the majesty and authority of a sovereign State has been insulted and contemned by the Govenor and authorities of a petty Territory it should seek remedy worthy of itself . . .

Besides, the Iowans had just called them "Pukes." People out on the frontier sometimes called Missourians "Pukes" and Missourians hated it.

"Death to the Pukes," soldiers in the Iowa army had cried as they marched toward Missouri.

For there was an Iowa army. There was also a Missouri army. Missouri and Iowa were having a war that December. It was as fine a bit of winter madness as the prairie has ever seen.

It may have been the longest war in U.S. history, running, as some authorities will have it, from 1836 to 1851. On the other hand, it may have been the country's shortest, for, in a sense, it stopped before it started.

The casualties were two haunches of deer meat, but they were buried with full military honors.

The war cost Missouri $20,000, raised by floating the state's first bond issue. Iowa, still a territory, requested $30,000 from the U.S. government to pay for its share, but Congress balked and the money was never appropriated.

Depending upon which state one favors, it was called the Iowa War, or the Missouri War. It was also called the Honey War because a contributing cause was the rustling of three bee trees. That act certainly added to the general crotchetiness on both sides, but even winter-weary Iowans and Missourians would not have had themselves a $50,000 war if there hadn't been more to it than that.

Basically, it was a border war over the boundary line between Missouri and Iowa and the story started some thirty-five years earlier, once again as winter was coming to the prairie.

In St. Louis, in November of 1804, the United States signed a treaty with the Sac and Fox Indians who ceded their land west of the Mississippi River and north of the Missouri River to a line that runs, roughly, along the present Iowa-Missouri border.

One Indian, however, refused to agree to the treaty. Black Hawk, a formidable Sac warrior with a cool and sober head, pointed out that the chiefs had not been sent to St. Louis to give away land, but to negotiate the release of an Indian held prisoner there. Forgetting their mission, Black Hawk charged, those chiefs "had been drunk the greater part of the time," and returned, much later, "dressed in fine coates . . . and medals."

So Black Hawk and his warriors continued to make life hot for the white men north of the Missouri

River to such a degree that the settlers had little time to worry about where the actual boundary of the territory was. In 1815, William Clark, he of Lewis and Clark fame, and by then Govenor of the Territory of Missouri, issued a proclamation dismissing the Sac, Fox, and Osage claims to the land, declaring, "The pretensions of other nations of Indians to lands lying within these limits being of very recent date, are utterly unsupported by those usages and that possession and prescription accustomed to found their territorial claims." Clark defined the northern "limit" generously, considerably north of the previous Indian line, running from 140 miles north of the mouth of the Kansas River (at the site of Kansas City) east to the Mississippi in a line that ran 10 miles north of present-day Ottumwa.

After the war of 1812 (which Black Hawk joined on the British side) white settlers began to move into the area north of the Missouri River, so in 1816, when Black Hawk finally gave up his opposition and affirmed the treaty of 1804, John C. Sullivan was appointed to survey and mark the northern border of Missouri. Not being quite so greedy as Governor Clark, Sullivan started at a point 100 miles north of the mouth of the Kansas River and ran the line along what he hoped was a parallel of latitude and marked it by blazing trees, building mounds, and driving stakes. However, "from want of proper care in making corrections for the variation of the magnetic needle," Sullivan's line veered north at the Des Moines River. There were now two more boundaries—the parallel intended and the line surveyed. Both lines were south of Clark's line.

Where was the border? To make matters precisely clear, when Missouri entered the union in 1820, the northern boundary line was described as the parallel of latitude "which passes through the rapids of the river Des Moines."

Clear? Well, not quite clear.

Boatmen on the Mississippi would have guessed the phrase to refer to the Des Moines rapids, marked on old maps, an eleven-mile stretch of rough water a few miles upstream from the junction of the Des Moines River and the Mississippi. A line run through any point in these rapids would have dropped the northern boundary of Missouri to the south of Sullivan's line. But where was the point in that eleven-mile stretch of water from which the line should be run? And was that what was meant by the "rapids of the river Des Moines"?

The questions began to be important as more settlers moved into northern Missouri and southern Iowa. They were a rough and motley crew, remembered by one of their contemporaries, an Iowa veteran of the Honey War, Alfred Hebard, as nomads who lived mostly by hunting, "bushwhackers . . . border ruffians . . . naughty Missourians . . . rude ramblers . . . in a locality where the moral element at the time had few attractions for well disposed people . . ." For the life of him, Hebard could not see why Iowans would want to settle there. But the area was rich in game and wild bee trees. The latter furnished not only the sole sweetening in the frontier diet, but beeswax, an important item in frontier trade. Bee hunting was business and the land along the border was one of the best places for wild bees. The valley along the Chariton River running some fifty miles north of the present border was even called the Bee Trace.

The "naughty Missourians" and the Iowans were beginning to jostle one another.

The Missouri state legislature ordered the border surveyed by Joseph C. Brown. Instead of trying to find the old blazes and mounds from Sullivan's survey and running the line eastward, Brown decided to use the "rapids of the River Des Moines" as his starting point and shoot a line westward. Ignoring the traditional Des Moines rapids on the Mississippi River, Brown chose to understand the phrase to mean rapids on the Des Moines River. After wading sixty-three miles up that river, he found a disturbance in the water at the Great Bend. These low water rapids disappeared after a rain, nevertheless Brown took them to be the rapids referred to in the state's charter and ran his line from them westward to the Missouri River, thus neatly giving the state of Missouri 2600 square miles more of highly desirable land than did the Sullivan line.

It is no surprise that the state of Missouri accepted Brown's survey, nor is it a surprise that settlers in the area who called themselves Iowans were unhappy with it. The following year, after the Territory of Iowa was separated from Wisconsin, a new commission was established to survey the boundary again. There were seats on the commission for three officials—one from Missouri, one from Iowa, and one from the U.S. government. Missouri, satisfied with the Brown survey, refused to appoint a commissioner and so the federal man, Albert M. Lea, and Dr. James Brown Davis, from Iowa, began the survey alone. The two men worked through October and well into November but sickness in the survey party and "the unusually early beginning of a rigorous winter" prevented verification of the full line. Lea, winter weary, concluded that good arguments could be made for any of four boundary lines, but recommended to the U.S. Congress that the old Sullivan line be accepted as a compromise that rather evenly divided the disputed land.

Missouri did not wait for Congress to act, but instead, in February 1939, the state legislature declared that Missouri's jurisdiction extended to the Brown line.

Spring and summer passed. Bees made honey and wax and bee hunters searched out the trees they stored it in. One of the hunters, a Missourian, crossed into the strip of disputed land and cut down three bee trees. Iowans said he had no right to them, no Missouri bee hunters allowed, and sued the rustler in an Iowa court. The judgement went against him and he was fined $1.50 in damages and costs.

In August, Sheriff Uriah S. "Sandy" Gregory, from Clark County, in northern Missouri, went to the only settlement in the disputed land, Farmington, to collect taxes from a group of people who were raising a house. They not only refused to pay taxes, but chased Sheriff Gregory out of town.

Back home, he made his report and it was passed on to Lilburn W. Boggs, governor of Missouri.

Governor Boggs, an uncompromising and opinionated man, is remembered in history for his infamous expulsion of the Mormons from the state and for having given orders to exterminate the Mormons if they did not submit. He was a hardheaded man, both figuratively and literally. One day after his retirement from office he was sitting at home, his back to the window, and a Mormon formerly in his employ tried to kill him, shooting directly at close range into the back of his head. The bullets, however, did not penetrate his skull and Boggs recovered from the wounds and went on to political glory in California.

Tough, stubborn frontier politician that he was, Boggs could hardly have been amused to hear that a Missouri sheriff had been chased by a bunch of Iowa carpenters.

Later in November, Governor Boggs issued a proclamation urging all officers to stand firm and do their duty and directed Sandy Gregory to go back to Farmington and collect taxes.

This time a large and excited crowd and the sheriff of Van Buren county, Iowa, were waiting for him. The Iowa sheriff briskly arrested the Missouri sheriff and hustled him off to jail in Muscatine, up to the north.

Winter winds and snow had begun to blow across

the prairie and Governor Boggs and Robert Lucas, governor of the Iowa Territory, began raising armies.

Governor Lucas had told his legislature early in November that the dispute might "ultimately lead to the effusion of blood." He was an old hand at bitter border disputes and knew what he was talking about. Before he had come to Iowa, Lucas was Governor of Ohio and had led 600 men to Maumee, where he faced 1,000 Michigan soldiers under the generalship of their governor. No one was killed in that, the Wolverine War, only because commissioners from Washington arrived at the last moment and restored the peace. But out across the Mississippi, Washington was far away and Lucas knew just what to do.

Lucas ordered Jesse B. Brown to raise the Iowa militia. General Brown stood six foot seven and had a reputation for high spirits. Once he had dispersed a tavern crowd by throwing into the heating stove a gunpowder keg that he alone knew to be empty, swearing lustily all the while that the population had lived long enough. Brown needed every inch of command and presence to be able to transform Iowa frontiersmen into an army.

A force of 1,200 was called up. Of that number there were 136 officers, ranging from four full generals down to a host of company commanders. But only about 500 showed up at Farmington for war, a state of affairs understandable when one reads the reminiscences of Hebard, the Honey War veteran who had such a low opinion of the border settlers. Hebard, writing some fifty years after the war, recalls

I found, on reaching my cabin . . . an unexpected document, nothing less than a commission from the Commander-in-Chief, appointing me captain of a military company to be raised within a certain defined beat . . . Recovering from a momentary amazement, I rode over to see and consult with my lieutenants. No matter what we thought, we agreed at once to drum up our beat. Couriers were dispatched to sound the tocsin in the remotest corners, proclaim the imminence of war, and call upon all able-bodied men to appear the following Monday at Billy Moore's blacksmith shop . . . Also to bring with them or report all war machinery within their reach . . . At the appointed hour, the Captain, with an old dragoon sword strapped to his side, made a brief speech, saying that all understood the situation as well as he did, but owing to the great difficulty of providing supplies, equipments and transportation at such an inclement season it was necessary to know first what our force would be. He knew that some could not go, others were disinclined and might risk disobeying orders. To test the matter he scratched a line in the light snow on the ground, and requested all who would go to come forward and "toe the mark." For several minutes no one moved. Presently, however, two sons of Erin, who probably found something somewhere to stir their courage, shoved the toes of their boots up to the line. The infection spread, another and another slowly ventured up, till finally a large majority were on the line, brave and hilarious. The Captain, nolens volens, was "in for it" now. The only thing to be done was to make ready and report as soon as possible. We agreed to meet the next Wednesday and see how near we could get to a starting point. Wednesday came and we straggled together again, but not in a very hilarious mood this time. Many had been painting what they were to leave behind. They fancied a lone cabin in the edge of a grove, with its early smoke rising straight to the clouds; the wood-pile at the door, consisting of a few saplings, half covered with snow, a dull axe leaning against it, waiting to be used; an old cow, with roached back, in the angle of a fence that enclosed the hay, waiting for attention. But where was the man whose duties were thus suggested? He was a hero now marching to the Missouri line, one hundred miles away, to reconstruct the disorderly, while the wife and children and the cow took care of themselves in a temperature below zero.

There was no money to arm the men with guns, so they brought their own weapons including blunderbusses, flintlocks, and swords at best. One man reported for duty with a plow coulter slung around his

The troops disbanded, turned their coats inside out, and wandered home, skylarking, burning down fences, and card sharping along the way. They made such a nuisance of themselves that when the Grand Jury next met, it indicted 100 of the war veterans for gambling.

While the ragtag troops from both sides had been massing on the border, delegations from Iowa and Missouri had met and drawn up a truce. One Thomas L. Anderson is said to have urged the acceptance of the truce to the court of Clark County, portraying the horrors of war and the blessings of peace with such eloquence that those hearing him wept. If so, he should have been present the night of December 15 when those citizens of Lewis County, directly to the south, met at Pemberton's hotel and passed their resolutions quoted at the outset. They were furious over the troops' return and wanted no part of any truce, condemning instead the "menial and begging policy instituted by certain modern school peace mongers."

With such touchiness still in evidence, it is a wonder that the truce held, but hold it did. And although various Missouri sheriffs continued, without success, to try to collect taxes and were sued in Iowa courts for their attempts, the troops were not called up again.

Both sides wanted the U.S. government to resolve the issue and during the early 1840s, Congress debated the border question in a desultory way, eventually, in 1844, calling for yet another survey, provided that the act would be approved by Missouri. Missouri, naturally, did not approve, for it had more to lose than gain by a new survey and it was not until 1845 when

Iowa became a state that the dispute was submitted to the Supreme Court.

Missouri argued before the court for the acceptance of the Brown line passing through the "rapids of the River *of* Dès Moines" at the Great Bend in the Des Moines River and Iowa stoutly urged a boundary on a parallel of latitude that passed through not those "riffles" but instead the "rapids of the River Des Moines" *of* the Mississippi River. It took the court four years to decide that the Des Moines River had only riffles, that the Des Moines Rapids were on the Mississippi, and that the Old Indian Line, the Sullivan line, was the proper compromise to mark the boundary. Then, in what has the appearance of judicial exasperation at the silliness displayed by both parties, the Court directed that the boundary should be marked by iron pillars every ten miles with "Missouri" engraved on the south side, "Iowa" on the north, and "boundary" on the east.

Those pillars, once cast, weighed as much as 1,600 pounds and were difficult to put in place. Roads and bridges had to be built to haul them in. In addition, it was nearly impossible to decide where to put them. Traces of the old Sullivan line of 1816 were eventually found, the magnetic error deduced, but it was further discovered that Sullivan's crooked line was not even consistantly crooked. So to mark the squiggles in the border, the surveyors drove wooden posts every mile between the iron posts.

It was not until 1851 that the commission finished its job and Henry Hendershot, commissioner, submitted the bill for the work. It was over $10,000 and Missouri and Iowa each had to pick up $3,000 of the tab. One Iowa legislator, reviewing expenses, objected to the $7.12 per diem charge for surveyors, especially since he himself only received $3.00 a day. Eying Hendershot, he protested mildly, "Well, Henry, I had lieve help you steal as any man, but I really think you are dipping a little too deep into the public crib."

And so ended the Honey War.

The clash of human events has sometimes been stimulus to artistic creation and if the greatness or smallness of the art produced has any relationship to that of the event, the Honey War can, perhaps, be judged by the poem that it inspired. It was published in the Palmyra Whig (of Missouri) in October 1839, after the bee trees were cut, but before the troops were called up. It was popular, in a modest way, in the 1840s and was meant, according to its author, John W. Campbell, to be sung to the tune of Yankee Doodle.

THE HONEY WAR

Ye freeman of the happy land,
    Which flows with milk and honey,
Arouse to arms, your poneys mount,
    Regard not blood or money.
Old Govenor Lucas, tiger like,
    Is prowling round our borders,

But Govenor Boggs is wide awake,
   Just listen to his orders.

Three bee trees stand about the line
   Between our state and Lucas,
Be ready all the trees to fall,
   And bring things to a focus.
We'll show old Lucas how to brag,
   And claim our precious honey,
He also claims, I understand,
   Of us three bits in money.

The dog who barks will seldom bite,
   Then let him rave and splutter;
How impudent must be the wight
   Who can such vain words utter.
But he will learn before he's done,
   Missouri is not Michigan.
Our bee trees stand on our own land,
   Our honey then we'll bring in.

Conventions, boys, now let us hold,
   Our honey trade demands it,
Likewise the three bits all in gold,
   We all must understand it.
Now in conventions let us meet,
   In peace this thing to settle,
Let not the tiger's war-like words
   Now raise too high our mettle.

Why shed our brother's blood in haste,
   Because big men require it?

Be not in haste our blood to waste,
   No prudent man desires it.
But let a real cause arise
   To call us into battle,
We're ready then, both boys and men,
   To show the true blue metal.

Now if the Govenors want to fight,
   Just let them meet in person,
For Govenor Boggs can Lucas flog,
   And teach the brag a lesson.
And let the victor cut the trees.
   And have three bits in money.
And wear a crown from town to town
   Annointed with pure honey.

And then no widow will be made,
   No orphans unprotected,
Old Lucas will be nicely flogg'd,
   And from our line ejected.
Our honey trade will then be placed
   Upon a solid basis,
And Govenor Boggs, where'er he goes,
   Will meet with smiling faces.

ABOUT THE AUTHOR

Sue Hubbell was born in Kalamazoo, Michigan. She is a commercial bee-keeper and a writer. Married, she splits her time among Washington, DC, the Ozarks of southern Missouri where her apiary is located, and the frequently unusual places to which her writing assignments take her.

Hubbell covers such natural phenomena as the lives of long-distance truckers, life in modern-day Guatemala, and the great New Madrid, Missouri, earthquake for such magazines as *The New Yorker* and *Smithsonian*. She is fondly remembered by many for the image-shattering *Hers* columns she wrote in the 1980s for *The New York Times*.

Her earlier books, *A Country Year* and *A Book of Bees* were chosen by *The New York Times Book Review* as Notable Books of the Year.